YOU CAN CHANGE THE WORLD!

**Everyday Teen Heroes
Making a Difference Everywhere**

MARGARET ROOKE

Forewords by Taylor Richardson and Katie Hodgetts

Jessica Kingsley *Publishers*
London and Philadelphia

D0062288

First published in 2019
by Jessica Kingsley Publishers
73 Collier Street
London N1 9BE, UK
and
400 Market Street, Suite 400
Philadelphia, PA 19106, USA

www.jkp.com

Copyright © Margaret Rooke 2019

Front cover image credit: Kara McHale.

Library of Congress Cataloging in Publication Data
A CIP catalog record for this book is available from the Library of Congress

British Library Cataloguing in Publication Data
A CIP catalogue record for this book is available from the British Library

ISBN 978 1 78592 502 3
eISBN 978 1 78450 897 5

Printed and bound in Great Britain

'A beautiful tribute to the power of youth and their driving passion to see and make change in the world. What we gain from these active young voices is that hope, not despair is on the move, and one small change sparks another.'
  – Amie Williams, Co-Founder and Executive Director, GlobalGirl Media

'This book is positive, impactful and vital. By reading this, you really can change the world.'
  – Eve Ainsworth, award-winning teen author

'As education editor of The Sunday Times I am fed up with hearing about Generation Snowflake. Here at last is a book that disproves that label. I loved reading these stories of 50 teenagers who have literally changed the world for the better through their efforts. Hurrah for the next generation – Generation Sunshine!'
  – Sian Griffiths, Education and Families Editor, The Sunday Times

'"Inspirational" is an over-used word, but this really is an inspirational book! Modest, practical and passionate, these stories should be given to every young person who has a heart and is wondering how to use it.'
  – Nick Luxmoore, school counsellor and author

'A step-by-step guide to changing the world, what's not to love? A great book for any teen wanting to turn passion into action.'
  – Dr Pooky Knightsmith, Vice Chair of Children and Young People's Mental Health Coalition, @PookyH

'A fantastic book that captures the work of young changemakers. Powerful and inspiring, a catalogue of real role models. It will make you want to chase your passion. After all what better cause is there?'
  – Matteo Bergamini, CEO and Founder, Shout Out UK, @ShoutOut_UK

'This book is truly an amazing read. It tells the beautiful stories of some absolutely astounding teenagers making the most of life. As a teenager myself these stories fill me with hope and show me that no matter how hard life can get as a teen, there's always a light at the end of the tunnel. And that even though sometimes you feel small and insignificant, you can make a difference.'

– Ben Roots, aged 17

'What an inspiration! If this doesn't get you dreaming, thinking and doing something about a better world, nothing will! The bold testimonies honestly help you realize how mighty the power of one is. These true stories really have a magic and force that is radical and captivating!'

– Rachael Dellaca, WA, Australia, aged 17

'I think this book is amazing as we always hear about the terrible acts of teenagers and forget about the good things that we can do. It reminds us that we have the power to make a difference even when people say we are too young to understand. I'm inspired to make a change.'

– Seren, aged 13

'I hope that this book will be widely read by teenagers. I think it shows that whatever life throws at them, especially in what are often such vulnerable and uncertain years, they are not alone; there is always a way forward, and there are others out there like them who know what they are going through. I hope this moving book will inspire other teenagers to feel better about themselves and encourage them to harness their passion and determination into a real force for good in this often difficult world.'

– Zelda West-Meads, Agony Aunt for You *magazine,* Mail on Sunday

In memory of my dad, Stan, who thought this book was a great idea;
Auntie Liz, who'd have loved it; and my friend Jane, teen hero of her time.

"When we start to act, hope is everywhere. So instead of looking for hope, look for action. Then the hope will come."

GRETA THUNBERG,
CLIMATE CHANGE ACTIVIST,
@GRETATHUNBERG

CONTENTS

FOREWORD

TAYLOR RICHARDSON,
15, Florida, USA
Activist, speaker, philanthropist and
aspiring astronaut

Today's teens know that age doesn't determine if someone
has wisdom. We don't need to ask for permission from the
adults 'in charge' or wait until we reach an arbitrary age before
determining that our opinions mean something. We're willing to
take a stand, use our voices and make an impact on the world as
we see it.

The great thing about this book is that the teenagers who tell
their stories show the rest of us what's possible. As teenagers, we
do what we see, not what we're told. The more positive examples
there are in the world that we hear about, the more teenagers will
follow along. When I see a teenager making change and expressing
what they see is wrong in society, it provides me with the fuel to do
exactly the same thing.

We are around other teens most of our waking hours so,
after a certain age, we tend to be influenced more by our friends
and classmates than our parents. Between class, extracurricular
activities, hobbies and social media, a teenager is interacting with

other teens more than 50 hours a week. The internet and social media have made it easier than ever to find people with shared experiences, no matter where they are in the world. This allows for a level and efficiency of mobilization that was not possible in past generations.

My peers are the next set of adults who will be in charge, and the earlier we start speaking our truth the more practice we'll have at it. I am someone who is quiet and reserved – people are amazed when I tell them this – and I have done interviews with major news organizations and spoken at international conferences. I'm still nervous before each of my speaking engagements but, with practice, I have learned the world is not going to end if I mispronounce a word every once in a while.

As teenagers we are not expected to be perfect. We have time to make mistakes, recover from them, and build the lives we want to live. That's why it's such a good time for fighting for the changes we want to see.

For all of us, life can be tough during teenage years. I have been bullied for my skin color and that was painful. But the sooner you become comfortable with who you are, how you look, how you sound and who you love, the more peace you can have inside. A friend once reminded me that you control your self-esteem, because it's how you feel about yourself, not what you think others think about you.

I was held back in second grade* and had to build my reading skills before I progressed at school. Despite this, I never let myself

---

*   Ages 7–8.

believe I was destined to fail. I had people in my life who let me know that I wouldn't be defined by one setback. My mom said she was going to buy more books and read with me every night, which she did. What I've done since that time will always define me more than what I couldn't do at seven years old.

What my mom did to help me with my reading is a great example of how the belief and support of another is sometimes all one needs to believe in themselves. Maybe that's one reason why I redefined my ADHD as 'Abundantly Different and Happily Divine!' I made the decision to celebrate myself because I was born this way. No one with ADHD should be ashamed of who they are. We need to learn what will help us in class, while taking a test, or working at home, and ask for help. If we don't, we are only hurting ourselves.

I've found most of my setbacks have turned into some of my biggest successes. My own difficulties with reading when I was young prompted me to organize a successful book drive and reading program for disadvantaged children called 'Taylor's Take Flight'. This led to me winning the Governor's Service Award in Florida. After this I was invited to a private screening of *Hidden Figures*, the film about African-American women at NASA, with First Lady Michelle Obama at the White House.

That screening and the lack of diversity I found when I attended Space Camp inspired my promotion of inclusion for all in STEM (Science, Technology, Engineering and Math). It's so important that no one believes they can't succeed in these subjects because of the color of their skin or their gender.

I created a fundraising campaign that raised $20,000 to sponsor youth screenings of *Hidden Figures*. I also inspired free youth screenings in 72 cities throughout 28 countries. This movement was proof that good intentions and hard work can lead to great results.

My own lofty goal is to become an astronaut. When I was younger, I would lie down outside and look into the night sky. I was fascinated with space and the stars. I imagined what was out in the universe. Now my attitude is, don't just dream it, do it. Whether one's interests are in STEM, the arts or anything for that matter, do not let the opinions of others restrict the ambitions you have for yourself. This book is filled with inspiring stories of teens who did not let barriers stop them from reaching their goals for themselves or for those around them.

For teenagers everywhere, the sky is our limit!

– Taylor Richardson (Astronaut StarBright)

@astrostarbright
@astronautstarbright

FOREWORD

KATIE HODGETTS,
23, Bristol, UK

Campaigner for UK Youth Climate Coalition, contributor to *The Ecologist*, co-organiser of Bristol Youth Strike 4 Climate, finalist in Global Youth Awards 2018

Teenagers and young people today have been labelled as the 'Snowflake Generation'. It's meant to be a criticism – that we are weak and take offence too easily – but I see it as positive and powerful. Snowflakes are individual; they are unique and complicated; they are amazing and when we join together, we form an avalanche; a disruption.

Teenagers have the capacity to be global change makers. This doesn't mean that they are always standing in the street shouting about what they believe. Change, empowerment and inspiration can happen in the most unconventional settings: through conversations in cafés, through writing blogs or social media posts or simply being kind in a world which can contain so much darkness. Every day young people can make the choice to look out for other people and all of this can form part of the change they want to see.

Everyone in this book, in their own way, is someone making that choice. Everyone is inspiring and showing the path to living a better life in a better world.

It's not always easy to take this path. As a teenager I felt the pressure to fit in, and that stopped me from engaging in activism for fear of judgement. It was only years later that I realized I was not alone when I reached out to other people in the UK Youth Climate Coalition and learnt how much stronger we are when we're together, pushing for change. This made all the difference to me.

Certainly I've experienced how the airbrushed world of social media can anaesthetise you to the world around you. It can separate you from the rest of life and lead you to value yourself by how many likes you have rather than the unique things that make you, you. We can spend so much time looking at our online persona, and not out at the world in front of us. Learning to step beyond this takes a lot of bravery but, as the teenagers in this book demonstrate, it's stepping outside of this bubble that makes people so impressive.

It takes bravery to be unashamed of who you are, to live authentically and work to do what's best for yourself and the world. This is exactly what I witness young people doing more and more.

When I was growing up I felt riled by the injustice I saw around me, from bullying to extreme poverty. I was desperate to do something but felt powerless. I couldn't even vote in elections, so it felt easier to carry on socialising, planning a conventional career and doing nothing.

We all need something that propels us into action and, when I left school, I went to a remote area of Morocco to teach English. I witnessed such desperate poverty there and simultaneously such rich happiness and it made me question both global inequality and what we strive for in modern life.

While I was at university I went to Tanzania and climbed Mount Kilimanjaro for the Hope for Children charity. I fell in love with nature and I learnt more and more about the damage we had done, to the people of the Global South and their environment, with the extraction of fossil fuels and minerals for our consumption.

This led me to campaign against climate change. Many people think climate change is just about rainforests and saving polar bears, but it is deeply political and a fight for justice. We in the Global North have lived a life of relative affluence at the expense of those in the South. It is these people who will bear the brunt of changes to the climate, including famine, drought and extreme weather. I felt a deep responsibility to challenge a system where oil and energy tycoons are capitalising on the future of those with less privilege.

So I joined the UK Youth Climate Coalition. For me it was such an empowering experience to stand shoulder to shoulder with these inspirational teenagers and young people. Since then I have campaigned with different groups, occupied a fracking site for three days, protested outside Parliament, given speeches at rallies and festivals, taken part in panel discussions and even became a finalist for the Global Youth Awards 2018. Anything is possible.

I was nominated for the award by my amazing anti-fracking team for implementing wellbeing and mental health initiatives as

I was watching young people face burnout. Mental stress is a real risk when you are dealing with the huge problems that the world is facing and looking after yourself is the most important thing we can do as we try to effect change.

I then got involved in co-organising the Bristol Youth Strike 4 Climate. It moved me to tears to see these young people taking a stand. The ripple effect these strikes have created in so many countries gives me such hope and optimism for the future.

My advice if you are reading this is to remember that change can be incremental. My own journey was a slow one. My friends were saying to me, 'Why are you always bringing down the mood? Can't we talk about parties and boys?' So I started to put my frustrations down on paper. Eventually I submitted some pieces to The Ecologist and they loved them, and started publishing my columns. The pen is definitely mightier than the sword. If you want to see change, I encourage you to write, talk, vlog, campaign, protest, march: inspiration comes in many shapes and sizes.

Conventional wisdom tells us that as you age you become 'older and wiser' but I think that real wisdom so often lies with the young. Perhaps cynicism can accompany age, which is why I have found many people dismissing me as a naïve, silly little girl when I've said that I want to change the world. As you get older it's easier to believe that power lies at the top and you no longer feel that miracles can happen. When you're young you have a sense of optimism; you can see the world as a blank canvas. You have an artillery of colours and can paint the world in any way you want. I love the spark of magic in young people that is captivating, though I believe older people can retain or re-find that spark of magic too.

It's important that adults don't underestimate young people. Give us support. Don't patronise us. Just look at Greta Thunberg. She's such a great example of how young people can step outside of the democratic process and force people to listen. She's our amazing Climate Beyoncé!

It's not young people who started wars or who created the messes we find ourselves in today. Let's put our faith in teenagers like the ones in this book, and let's celebrate and encourage all they can achieve that's great and powerful.

– Katie Hodgetts (KT Climate)

🐦 **@KTclimate**
📷 **@Bodha**
📷 **The UK Youth Climate Coalition: @UKYCC**

• • •

INTRODUCTION

If you are a teen and life can feel tough, this may be the book for you.

Here are more than 50 interviews with teenagers* who have told their stories to prove that changing their own lives – and changing the attitudes of others – is possible.

Some have begun to transform their local community or tackle national issues; some have helped others gain confidence and self-belief or have made dramatic shifts within themselves.

TV, newspapers and the internet tell us stories of teenagers who run riot and mess up. In this book, Amarni from London, who's 17, asks for a fresh light to be shone on the positive contributions that teenagers make. He says it would be great if as well as saying, 'This person died, this person got stabbed,' they said, 'This guy has made a track and it's gone viral.'

A meme I saw the other day sent out a similar message, 'MTV needs to stop doing TV shows like *16 and Pregnant* and start doing shows like *18 and graduated* and *21 and successful*.'[†]

---

*   Almost all of the interviewees are in their teens. Some are now in their early 20s but talk about what they achieved when they were younger.
†   Sarcastic Mama @SarcasticMa.

A recent Royal Society of Arts poll[‡] revealed that when asked to pick words from a list to describe teenagers, adults in the UK most commonly chose 'selfish', 'lazy' and 'antisocial'. The same research showed that, in fact, 84% of young people want to help others and 68% have done so through social action and volunteering. That's precisely what this book is about. Here you'll find stories of everyday teen heroes who may not make the news but breakdown the stereotypes and change the world for the better.

This book started out as a means to help teenagers who are going through a rough time, but it's turned into a read for anyone simply seeking some inspiration. Even those in this book who have lived through distressing experiences – and details of these can be tough to take in – show how their strength and resilience shine through.

Whether you read this from cover to cover, or flick through to find the stories that appeal to you most, you'll see that these teens have the power to take something difficult, painful or just plain wrong and turn it into something amazing. We can all do this in our own different ways. If you don't believe me, just take a look at the pages that follow…

> *If you'd like to email any of the young people whose stories are in this book, you can reach them using the address hello@jkp.com*
>
> *Margaret Rooke is on Twitter at @MargsRooke*

[‡] https://www.thersa.org/discover/publications-and-articles/reports/teenagency-how-young-people-can-create-a-better-world

1...

DEMANDING CHANGE

TRISHA,

18, Illinois, USA

"I developed a solution that allowed teenagers to pause, review and rethink before they posted anything online."

One day, at the age of 13, I came home from school to read an online story about a young girl named Rebecca. She had gotten into a feud with other girls at her school, who were constantly tormenting her online. They repeatedly cyberbullied Rebecca, and the abuse got so bad that she even transferred schools.

The bullying continued.

One day Rebecca couldn't take it anymore. She jumped from the top of a local water tower and ended her life.

When I read that story, I was so shocked. How could a girl younger than me be pushed to do this? We had lost an innocent girl: someone who had so much potential. A mother had lost her child. Why?

We live in a digital era, and social media has become a primary way we teenagers communicate with each other. I wondered what could have been done to prevent the cyberbullying and the tragedy that followed. I decided I didn't want to be a bystander. I wanted to be an upstander and stop this from ever happening again.

I started researching cyberbullying. Several social media sites were approaching cyberbullying through a reactive method that I like to call 'Stop, Block and Tell'. If a teen was being cyberbullied online, social media sites encouraged them to 'Stop' what they were doing, 'Block' the bully on social media and 'Tell' a parent or adult. However, there's a problem with this. Ninety percent of those who have experienced cyberbullying don't report it to anyone. They suffer in silence. I wondered why we were placing the burden on the victim. Also, why are we waiting to deal with the issue after it is done? Why are we not preventing it before the damage begins?

The main question that stuck with me was 'What is causing teens to post mean and hurtful messages online?' As a teen myself, I knew that teens are not inherently mean or bad people. I knew that I had to better understand our teen brain and the root cause of this behavior.

In my research, I came across a scientific study which compared the teenage brain to a car with no brakes. I learned that the portion of the brain which helps decide right from wrong is in the front of the brain. It is called the prefrontal cortex and does not develop fully until we reach our mid-20s. The study suggested that the teenager's brain is a work-in-progress and it may often cause teenagers to act on impulse. In the heat of the moment, teens may not consider the consequence of what they are doing.

I wondered why social media sites didn't guide teenagers to understand their actions, prompt them, help them realize the gravity of what they were about to post online. Suddenly, I realized that this itself could be an effective solution.

Armed with this research, I developed my idea, which I called ReThink – a solution that allowed teenagers to pause, review and rethink before they posted anything online. I conducted a scientific trial study at my local library for many months to understand the effectiveness of my idea. I used two software programs to measure the efficacy of a ReThink alert: one with

ReThink, and another without ReThink. If someone was posting something like 'You are so ugly. Go kill yourself,' an alert prompt would appear on their screen that says, 'Are you really sure you want to post this? This could be hurtful to them' or 'Is this message really you? Do you want to think before sending this message?' This gave them a moment to review what they were about to send. I found that when teenagers had a chance to pause, review and ReThink what they were about to post, 93 percent changed their minds and didn't post the hurtful message. The action was stopped before the damage was done.

I have always believed that the most complex problems often require simple solutions. As a freshman in high school, I knew I had to do something to get this idea in the hands of every teenager. A teacher suggested that I present my idea at an international science fair for teens. I was chosen as a Global Finalist in the Google Science Fair 2014, the first behavioral science project to be included.

This competition really launched me on to the global stage and gave me the platform to raise awareness about this issue and kick-start the 'ReThink' movement to stop cyberbullying. It gave me the opportunity to travel around the world, to London, New York and India, giving TED talks. I was invited to the White House and was recognized for my goals by President Obama.

In my travels I have spoken with thousands of teenagers. In many of these conversations, they talked about how they were deeply and emotionally invested in communication they had over social media and through technological devices. The consensus was clear: words online matter.

ReThink has now been introduced to more than five million students, and the technology is available in several international languages. The ReThink message has reached over 134 countries via the State Department's Share America initiative.

One of the best parts of being a teenager is believing in yourself and the idea that you are invincible. Growing up, almost every night, my mom would always tell me there wasn't anything I couldn't do. She'd tell me that life was an empty chapter for me to write and for me to make my mark. I might mess up, but I had nothing to lose.

All teens are passionate about something: music, art, science, law, politics, friends, communities, families. Every teenager has the potential to take their passions and achieve something meaningful. I truly believe that by channeling a passion into something unique, the world can be made a better place. I don't consider myself to be a talented genius – I have no special intelligence – but I have a dogged determination to leave the world a better place than when I found it.

To hone these passions, I've invested my time in a space that I care deeply about: arming girls and women with 21st-century technology and coding skills so they too can make their technological ideas a reality. In my experience teaching women these skills in a number of organizations, including Girls Who Code and Commit2Change, what I've found is that beyond coding I'm teaching them to be brave and helping them learn to go for what they want, even if failure is a possibility.

My message to all teens and tweens is to have faith in yourself. It's so easy to get down on yourself. Instead, lead with your strengths. You have a passion; you have a dream; chase after it and ignore all the naysayers. Turn into the one person who will always support you and that's yourself.

TRISHA

@rethinkwords
@TrishPrabhu

"You have a passion; you have a dream; chase after it. Turn into the one person who will always support you and that's yourself."

LUCY,

17, Sheffield, England

"I worded a petition about banning eggs from caged birds at Tesco and collected 280,000 signatures. To see this huge reaction was incredible."

Chickens didn't massively interest me until I was 12, when I happened to meet a flock of hens on a farm. I became particularly attached to one specific hen, who was injured. I was amazed at how interesting she was. I noticed how complex these animals are and was fascinated with how they interact with each other and with people. I had never realized any of this before.

We started calling her Mrs Hen. I carried her around a lot and spent a lot of time with her, hoping she would soon recover.

Purely out of interest, I started looking at how hens are treated commercially, and I began to learn about the different tiers of farming. I found out about the conditions experienced by caged hens: farming behaviour that seemed so stark compared with the life of the flock I had got to know. I started writing letters to supermarkets and politicians about these terribly cramped conditions. Quickly, I realized how little the letters were being taken notice of. Still today I have these folders full of letters with answers that would say something along the lines of 'Sorry you are unhappy'.

The more I found out about the issue, the harder it was to think, 'I can't be bothered.' The more they said, 'No, we can't help you,' 'No, we are not interested,' the more I was fuelled with this need to do something.

#NoMoreCages

My family has always had animals at home. I think pets are incredibly helpful; they bring you back to who you are and help you deal with stress. As a child, they can give you so much.

When I started campaigning, my life changed. I came to realize that a degree of respect and care for animals is not seen as being as important as how we interact with other people. At school they say we need to be kind to each other, but being kind to animals is not part of the national curriculum. Domestic animals are abused as well as animals at commercial farms. To me, it's so straightforward: don't hurt animals.

The campaign has been ongoing ever since I was 12. Looking back, you forget how much you put into these things. Letters back and forth. After a while I was surprised they replied, but even as my pile of paperwork grew, I knew that very little was really changing. These were just letters put at the bottom of the pile in the head offices, especially because they were from someone my age.

Then I saw someone do a local petition online and I thought I might just give it a go. To be honest, I would have been happy to collect just 100 signatures. I worded a petition about banning eggs from caged birds at Tesco and within hours there were hundreds of signatures. It was terrifying – but good terrifying! Amazing! I'd always known this was an issue many people cared about, but to see this huge, instantaneous reaction was utterly incredible.

The more the numbers kept going up, the more shocked I was. People were commenting from thousands of miles away. I still can't get my head around the number of people my petition reached. In the end, I sent 280,000 signatures to Tesco.

While the petition was still live, I started a letter-writing campaign and over 800 letters were sent; some people wrote their own messages, others used my suggested stock message. I had spent so many hours and days writing letters on my own, so there was something very special about the idea of such huge number of letters arriving at the headquarters.

One of the main elements of most of these letters was a section asking Tesco to meet with me to discuss the campaign, giving recognition to the scale of how many thousands were part of it. When I received the email from Tesco saying they were willing to meet me, I was completely delighted. I desperately hoped they would agree but, being as it is such a huge company, it was hard to expect anything at all.

I met with Tesco's Head of Agriculture and a Community Manager. I tried not to focus on exactly who I was meeting or how important they were. It was just about the issue. I knew the meeting could be overwhelming if I let it be, but I was so absolutely focused on getting them to make a change, or at least recognize the issue.

My mum came with me as I was still only 14, but I would have gone in on my own. I was excited more than anything – very clear about what I wanted to say.

What I didn't want was to go in there and them try to pacify me and tell me, 'Well done on the petition; now go home and stop it,' but, to their credit, they didn't just treat me like a child on a school trip.

I said to them, 'Regardless of the outcome of this petition, I will keep going. I will carry on.' I said, 'I'm not pulling back on the campaign.' I didn't for one minute get the impression they were considering any immediate change. Since its early stages, the campaign seemed to spark the interest of the media and we had a

Radio 4 reporter with us who was waiting outside. Tesco agreed to do an interview, but they didn't talk a lot about the issue of caged hens' eggs. They said they valued customer feedback as they were a customer-driven business.

I didn't hear anything for a while. Then a few weeks later they put out a press release which talked about ending the sale of eggs from caged hens. I was shocked and completely elated. I first heard the announcement during school time and I made sure to tell everyone who had shown their support for the cause – as well as calling my mum!

Sainsbury's were already stocking only free-range eggs, so I switched the pressure on to two other major supermarket chains in the UK, Asda and Morrisons. I knew because Tesco was a key market leader, its decision meant the others were more likely to follow. I launched that petition and in a week the numbers reached 180,000. The first one had created so much momentum. The charity Compassion in World Farming joined in, applying pressure to these specific retailers; so did the animal protection charity, the RSPCA. Other welfare organizations were also calling for change.

I did the whole social media thing as I knew many supporters of the petition would send messages on Facebook and Twitter. Social media can be a revolutionary tool in engaging people and uniting opinions. It has the capacity to have such an amazing impact and within a week those supermarkets made the same pledge as Tesco.

I had gone into overdrive, but it was important to me that the campaign never became aggressive, violent or confrontational. I just put forward what I saw to be logical and right.

The 'big four' supermarkets had either made the pledge or already operated with a policy against the sale of caged hens' eggs. Several smaller supermarkets, such as Aldi and Lidl, followed suit and also made public commitments. Almost every major supermarket agreed that the eggs would be phased out. This can't happen overnight, but they have all agreed to make the change.

During my GCSEs in the summer, I had to let the campaign settle down slightly, but there are several issues I'm looking to get engaged with. Despite the ending of sales of whole shell eggs from caged hens, the fact remains that many eggs used as ingredients, for instance in cakes, may still be sourced from these systems. To me, this is a major issue. Raising awareness of the need for early education in basic animal welfare will also always be one of my main priorities. I'm so glad I found campaigning, even if it was almost by accident. I love everything that comes with it, even public speaking. When I'm older, I'd really like to go down the track of working for social change. Recently I was completely honoured to have joined International Aid for the Protection and Welfare of Animals as an ambassador. Through this and other avenues I'm hoping to create a new and desperately needed awareness of the global plight of animals. Conservation is so important and I truly believe if we don't act now we may be facing a future with very little left to protect.

There must be something about being a teenager that makes me feel that this is a great point to look around and think, 'Is this the kind of world I want I want to grow up in?' I think my age helped me. Everything seemed so clear to me. I didn't let myself overthink what I was doing. The change was important to me and this let me shut out the criticism: people saying, 'She must have parents on the Tesco board,' or presuming I was a figurehead, not doing any of the work myself. If they had a valid argument, I would spend time thinking about that, but I didn't let personal comments get in the way of achieving something so incredibly important. In several cases, if people made personal remarks, there would be a thread of wonderfully supportive comments below to counteract them.

Along with the massive amount of support and huge positivity, I saw, unfortunately, that there will always be people who doubt what you're doing. The difficulty is getting people to engage with an issue that they feel is 'insignificant' or 'pointless' or even 'stupid', but you can never allow these voices to change your beliefs, to chip away at any determination that you have. I will always be proud that I became a campaigner and grateful that I met the wonderful Mrs Hen. Sometimes the smallest moments can spark the most incredible changes.

LUCY

 @LucyGavaghan
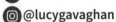 @lucygavaghan

> "Social media can be a revolutionary tool in engaging people and uniting opinions. Sometimes the smallest moments can spark the most incredible changes."

PARRY,

21, Devon, England

"It's not fair that children will grow up with dirty beaches and have to worry about something floating past them in the water."

Since I was a little kid I have lived by the sea. I go surfing and the ocean means a lot to me. It helps me when I'm stressed or if something's not right in my life. Even on a good day, if you go to the ocean, it just makes everything feel better. Being on the water clears your head; you can focus on yourself and what you are doing at that very moment. When you surf, you have to be very aware of what you're doing. I have surfed around the world and I know those waves can kill you.

From what I've seen, living near the sea makes everyone happier, in the summer or in the cold, horrible days of winter. The ocean helps you see how small you are and how small your problems are.

There's a local project here called the Wave Project that was built by a friend of mine and is backed by the NHS to help people with mental illness through surfing. I helped out there when I was young. One person had been scared of water to the point where he couldn't get in the shower. He had to wash out of a sink with a cloth and, for his first two sessions, he sat on a beach watching other people surf. By the third session his life was totally changed and he wasn't scared of water. He lived a completely normal life. So I've seen how water has the power to change lives. That we need to preserve it and keep it clean makes complete sense to me.

Ever since I've been surfing, I have been aware of plastic in the ocean. When I was 16, I did the National Citizenship Service and you do a project for four weeks with them. Mine was to do with clearing the ocean of plastic. After this they helped me to start building my own project.

I started my project with a friend, taking inspiration from other projects like Surfers Against Sewage and #2minutebeachclean. We began by running beach cleans and now we've moved on to going into schools, talking to kids. Our message is 'The next time you go to a beach, take a couple of minutes to pick up after yourself – and tell everyone else how important this is.' If everyone spent two minutes picking up litter from the beaches, more time would be spent doing this than has elapsed since humans have been on the planet.

These children are the next generation. Our goal is that they will tell their parents what we've said and tell their parents not to drop things on the beach. If you go to school and show them what's happening, no one will have to spend their life picking up litter. Pick up a few pieces and the ocean is much cleaner and much safer for everyone else.

I now work as a surf instructor and teach a lot of children. I want them to share the joy the ocean brings me. It's not fair that they will grow up with dirty beaches and have to worry about something floating past them in the water; they should have the right to enjoy it just as we have.

We have a small island near us called Lundy Island. It's the most biodiverse place in the UK, a big exploration zone for fishing, and it has seals, puffins, dolphins and the occasional basking shark. A big part of the local economy relies on tourism there, including wildlife cruises. We also have the largest working harbour in the South-West in Ilfracombe. Taking away wildlife would have a massive impact on the local community. If marine life is dying, 80 per cent of industry is gone. The further inland you go, there is more agriculture, but on the coast, where I live, it is all tourism and fishing, with the odd farm.

David Attenborough's TV programme *The Blue Planet* really helped to explain how big the problem of plastic is in our oceans. If someone comes down from Birmingham on holiday and sees a stunning white sand beach, they may not be aware what is happening. I think the majority of people are pretty good, and people are making more of an effort to carry rubbish with them to the bins. We can't persuade everyone to do this, but we don't want marine life to die. They were here before us.

PARRY

"If everyone spent two minutes picking up litter from the beaches, more time would be spent doing this than has elapsed since humans have been on the planet."

AMIKA,

18, London, England

"I read that girls were missing school for a week because they had their period and couldn't afford sanitary towels or tampons. I thought this was something everyone ought to be talking about."

An article on the BBC Schools website said that girls were missing school for a week because they had their period and couldn't afford sanitary towels or tampons. They had to choose to use socks or toilet paper or miss out on school.

I read this and was appalled. I know what it's like to feel stressed about missing a couple of days of school, especially in the run up to GCSEs or A levels, knowing how much that would leave me to catch up on when I got back.

Before I saw the article, I had never heard of the term 'period poverty'. As soon as I heard about it, I thought this was something everyone ought to be talking about. The government wasn't coming up with solutions or addressing the problem, so I started a petition on Change.org, asking for free menstrual care for all girls entitled to free school meals. I honestly thought that this made perfect sense. I thought nobody will be opposed to this.

I talked to my family and friends and this made sense to them too. I had hoped to get 50 signatures over a couple of weeks. In fact, I got 2000. Now I have more than 270,000. There is so much support, but period poverty is still something that not enough people have heard about and this needed to change.

My instincts were right. People's immediate response when they hear about it is 'What can I do to help?' I started organizing events using Instagram and Twitter. We organized a peaceful protest in December, right outside the Prime Minister's bedroom, and 2000 people came. We had amazing speakers including Daisy Lowe and the MP Jess Phillips. I didn't know how many people would come but I told my friends and they told their friends. It really took off.

The taboo around periods is ridiculous and the response to what we were asking for was amazing. When the petition was so successful, I naively expected a good response from the government. Nothing happened, but in March 2018 they announced that they'd allocate £1.5 million from the tampon tax fund – the money gained from putting aside the VAT from sanitary products – to help tackle period poverty, in addition to supporting the most vulnerable and disadvantaged girls and women, so that was one step forward. They also made a long-term pledge for VAT-free menstrual products.

Unfortunately, the government was still arguing that parents need to budget in order to cover the cost of sanitary protection, but these girls can't go to their parents and give them the choice of paying for food or pads. Many feel there's a stigma or taboo about discussing periods, which means they can't talk to their parents or their teachers at school. Sometimes teachers give girls their own pads, but that's not fair on them.

My family is quite open about periods. They have never been a hidden thing; they are just seen as part of life. They all encourage me with the campaign; my grandfather has been especially supportive. The more I campaign, the more ridiculous it seems that there is a taboo. It's so obvious that periods are a normal bodily process and it's ridiculous if we can't talk about them. Periods should be celebrated. They are the reason we can reproduce. They are not something to be embarrassed about.

At my primary school I had no education around periods. I remember the teachers saying, 'If anyone needs pads, they are in the teachers' toilets.' I didn't know what they were talking about. My mum had started young, so she sat me down one day and explained. I remember thinking, 'Why don't girls younger than me feel OK about talking about them?'

I still think there is a huge gap in education. There's a lot that needs to be changed in the way the education system deals with periods. After finishing my A levels I continued to raise awareness about my campaign. I went to New York to an event at the Bill and Melinda Gates Foundation, where I was one of three award winners, winning the campaign for FreePeriods. I knew I would continue with the campaign for as long as it took to achieve my goal. Then after university I want to work in human rights.

I think it's so important that teenagers don't shy away from taboo topics or things you think people don't want to know about. No issue is too small.

To succeed, you need to be confident. I started this campaign from my laptop at home. The internet has given people such an opportunity to connect with people using social media and the internet and make your voice heard. The more I have worked on this, the more confident I have become.

I have found that the support has been overwhelmingly positive, but there are always a few who post 'Why are you talking about periods while I'm eating my breakfast?' and 'Periods are disgusting.' Others say, 'I'm sure everyone can afford sanitary products. Surely they can find a pound.' This shows the level of ignorance. People are unaware there is such a great gulf between the rich and poor.

Credit: Alice Skinner

I would like to thank the BBC for opening my eyes to this issue. Also, my school was really supportive. I had to reschedule lessons and they changed my exams times so I could address a conference in America. Once I got an email asking me to go on the ITV news at one o'clock that day, and school was amazing. They let me miss a lesson and they are proud of what I've done.

I spoke at an international Facebook conference about safety online. Everyone on the panel had achieved things for the good through social media. We were all saying, 'It can be used for good.'

Then the government announced that there would be free sanitary protection in primary and secondary schools and colleges. They had listened to the campaigners. I was really thrilled. I think this is a hugely important and significant pledge and it means that no teenager will have to compromise their education because they have a period and can't afford period products.

We still have a huge amount of work to do to battle the ridiculous stigma around periods, that is so often culturally entrenched. We need to stop with the shame and embarrassment that we often feel when we talk about them. I think once we achieve that, and periods are a subject that men, women, boys and girls talk about freely and without reticence, then we will be a step closer towards achieving gender equality. It seems a long way off, but we are making progress.

There are so many issues that we can help to highlight and address. To me, this campaign is evidence that a teenager can elicit change in government policy. Age shouldn't stop anyone from believing that they can make the changes they want to see. We need to shout for the things that matter to us.

AMIKA

@AmikaGeorge

#FreePeriods

www.freeperiods.org

"It's so important that teenagers don't shy away from taboo topics or things you think people don't want to know about. No issue is too small."

FERLIN,

18, Cape Town,

South Africa

"We work to support other girls and to protect each other from violence and its repercussions. I think I have always had this ability in me to represent others and be a leader."

Gangs mostly rule in Manenberg, our area of Cape Town. One moment you have peace and quiet; the adults can enjoy their time outside and the kids can play. As soon as the shooting starts, the area clears so quickly it's like no one exists.

I have many bad memories as a young girl. I've witnessed bad things happening. More than once I've been caught in crossfire when gangsters were having a shootout. I've been going to school, getting myself an education, when I've found myself in this situation. The burden that I carry with these memories is a heavy one.

There have even been shooting incidents inside school. I remember when I was 10, the gangs broke into my school. One of my friends was terrified. She lived in an area with a great deal of violence. She ran into a cupboard and hid to make sure nothing happened to her. I knew it wouldn't be a good thing to panic and I decided to try to calm everyone down. It was really hard to calm down young kids, but eventually I managed it.

Even though violence is part of our daily lives, I think I have always had this ability in me to represent others and be a leader. I grew up with my mother and my grandmother. My mum is always really supportive and there for me. My grandmother was verbally abusive and said a lot of things that pushed down my confidence. I had to learn to express how I felt at any moment.

When I was 10, I joined with some other girls to set up an organization called BRAVE. We work to support other girls and to protect each other from violence and its repercussions. We knew we had to do something. We wanted to give ourselves a voice and speak about what life is like for young girls. Working with

BRAVE helped me to overcome the challenges I was facing in my own community and in my own household. I gained the skills of leadership and the confidence to stand up for what's right. I knew I had a great support system, a true sisterhood behind me.

One big thing we achieved is to help raise funds to build a new junior school. When I was there, the school was made of wood. Now it's made of brick and the school feels protected. It's safer. The kids are not exposed to violence in the same way that we were there. I still visit the junior kids with other members of BRAVE, to help them learn to be strong people and strong leaders. It feels good to be able to give back.

Another of our projects involved asking local artists to create beautiful mosaic benches all over Cape Town, not just in our district. There are now more than 50 'safe space benches' – places you can go and sit if you face problems at home, school or anywhere else. You can sit there if you want someone to reach out to you. The benches have positive, motivational messages on them, and a phone number to call if anyone needs help.

We have also created a WhatsApp group as we needed an easy way to contact each other. It's a great support system. I was in great danger once on my way to a BRAVE meeting; I was mugged. This guy took out a knife and threatened to hurt me if I didn't hand over my cell phone. That's how difficult it is to be a woman in our community. I had no choice but to give it up. I went to the nearest house and used a phone there and contacted the WhatsApp group to tell everyone what had happened.

Despite all our efforts, there is an ongoing threat of violence here and we did once lose one of the girls who was part of BRAVE. It was heart-breaking. It was a really terrible thing to lose such a great person.

In her memory, as well as for the sake of the rest of our generation, we have to keep fighting for what we believe in. Nine of us were fortunate to speak at the UN about defeating violence. We've met our country's justice minister. My goal is to meet the President of South Africa to see what he can do for us. I will always be a part of what I am doing now. It's made me the person I have become.

Poverty is one of the causes of violence. The gang members believe shooting each other will solve the problem, but it won't. I believe if we educate them about how much their violence affects the rest of the people, if we tell them about young girls not feeling safe, we can make a difference. Education is the key to overcoming the gang culture in our community.

Being a teenager is a great time to make changes to our world. This is the most flexible time of our lives; we adapt more easily to things. We can become great leaders and remain like this for the rest of our lives. Teenagers are social people and we can make sure we spread the word effectively and connect with other young people. My dream is that in the future we will be even more supportive to each other. We will relate with each other as if we are each other's mother or daughter. This is how great change can be made.

FERLIN

@BRAVE.RockGirl
#instaBRAVE2018
#brave_rockgirl
www.brave-girl.org

"Teenagers are social people and we can make sure we spread the word effectively and connect with other young people."

HAMPTON,

23, New York, USA

"I go to Black Lives Matter rallies. You get to hear people's stories and listen to their experiences."

One evening when I was 17, I was running from my friend's house to home and the police stopped me. No crime had been reported by anyone, but they were trying to figure out if I was a criminal who'd just stolen something from my neighbours. They were chancing it.

I remember at the time feeling vulnerable but not really threatened. They asked me for my ID and ran me through the system to see if there were any warrants out for my arrest. It seemed very weird as I was right outside my house. At the time I wasn't that upset but then, when I talked about it to my parents, they said it wouldn't have happened if I was my friend, who was white, and I was like 'What?' That definitely made me feel more upset.

I'm around 6 ft 1 now. I think I would have been 5 ft 11 then and I was a little more stocky. I could have looked somewhat older than 17, but not a lot older.

In my teenage years I became aware of more and more violence towards ethnic minorities, especially African Americans. It made me feel uneasy.

My parents raised me to know there was unfairness, but it really hit me when Trayvon Martin, who was about my age, was shot in Florida by this guy George Zimmerman in 2012. That was an event that got me. He was a high school kid who was walking to his father's house and he got stopped by this guy who was a part of the neighbourhood watch. He shot the kid, who was 17.

I was at my house eating dinner with my parents when I heard it on the news. I remember the impact this had. I remember feeling I had to be a lot more careful because I didn't know how the people I was near to on the street would react to me. I had to be careful of what I was wearing, how I look, what time I walk down the street, what I do.

I wasn't angry then – I didn't process what it all meant – but as the years went on I started to feel more upset about having to change how I act to make other people feel comfortable.

I have grown up in a privileged area. I do think this has made things different for me than they are for a lot of other African Americans. I know that I speak in a way that makes people feel comfortable with me from the start. This also makes me aware of the unfairness.

Of course a lot of events I had learned about from the past had an effect on me. In 1955 there was the Emmett Till hanging. He was a 14-year-old boy who was accused of offending a white woman in a grocery store and was lynched. Just one of the many hate crimes committed.

These are the reasons why I go to Black Lives Matter rallies. To me it is important to go along and see how issues affect other people, including those from less privileged areas. I just think it's good to go because you get to hear people's stories and listen to other people's experiences.

Because I go to the rallies I've seen a lot of white people support Black Lives Matter as well. It's heartening. It's very heartening. Some people I talk to about Black Lives Matter think it's too political and some people are scared they may be singled out if they take part. People from well off areas are often afraid about how they will be viewed in the community where they live. But I think going along allows you to understand other points of view and where they are coming from. Important on all fronts.

One example, I don't understand why people are so against sportsmen and women 'taking the knee' during the national anthem. I think they have every right to do it. There are a lot of military people who think that's all right to do. It's not a protest against the country; it's bringing awareness about the position of black people in society. It's a peaceful protest.

I think violence against black people is being reported more and that's a good thing. It's becoming more and more visible. I hope it will bring more attention to what's going on and stop the violence happening so often. My parents grew up through segregation, so these things were more normalized for them. I know they hoped my brothers and I wouldn't go through the same feelings they have. They raised me to be someone who joins in, who becomes part of what you believe in, and that's what I do.

HAMPTON

"I don't understand why people are so against sportsmen and women 'taking the knee' during the national anthem. It's not a protest against the country."

2...

NEVER
GIVING UP

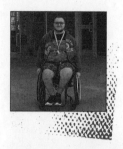

ALEX,

18, Calgary, Canada

"On my fifteenth birthday I broke my spine in four places. I have had to build myself new ambitions."

In Calgary, in the foothills of snow-covered mountains, the kids here are always sliding up and down the hills. You get hurt all the time but it's super-fun. On my 15th birthday, 21 December 2015, I decided to go tobogganing with my friends.

It's legal to toboggan on certain hills; on the other hills you are not supposed to, though people do it anyway and on that day I did too. I didn't have all the wisdom in the world and it was a poor decision. I hit a patch of ice, lost control and went headfirst into a wooden post.

My spine was fractured in four places. I knew instantly I would never walk again.

Luckily for me, I have very strong-willed parents. Failure is not an option. I knew, no matter what, I had to keep pushing and keep fighting for whatever I could achieve in life. I had always been taught if you fall off the horse you get back on the saddle. It's like, shit happens, what's next?

Before the accident, I didn't have an extraordinary life. I played the bagpipes. I took part in every sport under the sun, was in the army cadets, goofed off. I could have been anyone.

After the crash, everything changed. I was unconscious for a few seconds. Then I woke and the first thing my friends said was 'Are you going to get up and walk off, stay there for a few minutes, or shall we call an ambulance?' I thought, 'I can't feel my legs.' I knew it would be the ambulance. I knew instantly it was something major. I broke down and started screaming to my friends, 'I'm not ready to live like this. I can't live as a cripple.'

The next three to four days were a blur. When I first got to hospital, they were poking me with all sorts of needles. I was highly drugged and in a lot of pain. After a spinal cord injury, the parts you can feel are highly sensitive to touch. Not fun. Every nurse in the hospital was keeping me awake so they could do as many tests as possible, finding out how much was wrong with me.

I was not allowed to eat or drink anything for three days because they were concerned that chunks of my spine had damaged my oesophagus. Mum had to dab a sponge on to my mouth and that was the only water I had. Then a test that tasted disgusting showed there was no damage to my oesophagus and Mum forced me to eat and drink, though by then I'd lost my appetite.

I was 15 but I was 5 ft 11 and 150 pounds. This means I was man-sized and I didn't fit in the bed at the children's hospital. They were giving me child-size doses of morphine that were not cutting it for me. Thankfully, one of nurses said, 'Why don't we weigh him and give him enough morphine for his weight?' I was also moved to an adult hospital.

After I'd had surgery, and when the painkillers started to work, my psychological health went up. I still had my life, and with physio and occupational therapy I was slowly improving. Then there wasn't anything left to heal and the pain became psychological. I had no sense that I was progressing.

A month or two before I left the hospital, they gave me a therapist. However, the truth is that for the most part I had to deal with the psychological part of my injury alone. I have a great support system, but a lot of it fell on me.

I wanted to graduate with my year group, so, two to three weeks after the injury, I started doing online correspondence courses in my hospital bed. After this I did physio and occupational therapy until three in the afternoon, then I'd have one or two visitors until six, and then it was schoolwork again until late at night. Because I was in hospital for 19 weeks, that was the only way I would get to graduate on time. I'm so happy I did it, but it was tough.

I remember having Christmas in my hospital room. My parents bought a little plug-in tree. People were coming in, wishing me Merry Christmas. I think it was a bit sad and a bit happy: happy because it was Christmas and sad because I was in hospital and I was broken.

I gradually learned how to live in a wheelchair. I was starting a new school that year, and I arrived there a few months late when I was finally out of hospital. I found that everyone knew my name: a little bit odd as I didn't know anyone else's. I had been interviewed on TV to warn people to 'look before you leap' – not to go on unsafe runs – but I hadn't realized this would mean everyone knowing who I was.

Because I'd missed all those months, it felt as if I had missed the time to make friends. Everyone was nice to me and I had everything I needed to succeed, but throughout my time there I only had two close friends.

What I found particularly difficult was knowing when the rugby team was playing. I had played rugby for six years and it was my favourite sport. It was really tough to see other people doing what I should have been able to do.

The absolute hardest thing was that I always wanted to be a soldier, serving in the armed forces, going to military college and becoming an officer. They will never take me now because I am in a wheelchair. The chance of me working for them at all is very low. If Canada was ever attacked on its own soil, I would be unable to protect myself and would take someone out of the fight to help me, so I wouldn't even be allowed to work on a base.

I have had to build myself new ambitions, and in 21 days I'm moving to Lethbridge, one of the top colleges, to train to be a teacher.

This is because I have had so many teachers who have played a positive role, mentoring me. If I was to be a businessman, I wouldn't be able to make those changes in someone else's life. As a teacher, I will be able to influence young people. A lot of teachers care, but the ones that totally care are the ones that make the deepest impact on you. Above and beyond. The ones that think of you as one of their own children. That's how I want to be. I want to give back to the teachers who gave so much to me.

I have always loved military history, so I want to teach social studies – pretty much history, in fact. It's all part of my drive to give something back. I was a pretty cocky teenager before my injury; a little full of myself. I didn't think of others all that much. After my injuries I was humbled. It's hard to be cocky in a wheelchair. The accident has helped my humanity and I'm in a really good place right now.

I have a great family, I'm fairly successful for my age, I have an amazing girlfriend. We had dated before my injury for three weeks, then we broke up. She came to visit me after I broke my spine and we started talking again. We decided to make a go of it. It's ended up working out really well for the both of us.

I have a lot in my life and soon I will be living at college, away from home, completely independently. I'm always going to have bad days, but I believe that no one person's problems are worse than anyone else's. I have more good days than bad days. Sometimes I seek help. Most of the time I get in my own head and get myself back up.

I have been a peer mentor with the spinal injury group in Alberta, talking to people while they are still in hospital, helping them to realize their life isn't over. It's an immensely rewarding experience. I did a fundraiser for the group a month after getting out of hospital – a wheelchair marathon. I did 10K in an hour and the next year I cut that time by more than a half, finishing in around 28 minutes.

The biggest fundraiser was held in my church – a massive event that raised $100,000. The church came behind me and the city came behind me and supported me. We were all surprised by how much what happened to me has touched people.

Then I did one last fundraiser in 2016, run by my school, and we raised $20,000. I donated half of the money back to the school to say thank you for all they had done for me. I told them I wanted it to go to each core subject to spend on something fun for the students.

One of my proudest moments was at my graduation. I had been fitted into an exoskeleton, so I could walk across the stage, and no one knew I was going to do this, not even my dad. A lot of people came up to me and went, 'That was inspiring.' I don't think until that day I realized how much of an inspiration I was to the kids in my class. I think my injuries have taught them that no matter what you are going through, you're going to be fine; you're going to make it.

Right now, I'm trying to live a normal teenage life. I'm not trying to be special, just trying to live my life. I work in a locally owned shop. It's very difficult to find jobs as a teenager, especially when you're in a wheelchair, so it's amazing they had faith in me.

I think things happen for a reason; my injury happened for a reason – so that I can help other people. It's been difficult for my parents. This is definitely not something they wanted to happen, but they are very strong, and because they are strong I'm strong.

I always have hope that tomorrow will be better than today, no matter what has happened. The injury teaches me a lot; it makes me better than I was. It has forced me to mature past my years. I have so much perspective now that it is too hard for me to be a selfish teenager. I have seen too much to think only about myself.

ALEX

@aj.mcewan115

> "I knew, no matter what, I had to keep pushing and keep fighting for whatever I could achieve in life. My injury happened for a reason — so that I can help other people."

HECTOR,

19, Valladolid, Spain

"I had the opportunity to dance in London in a *pas de deux*. Then I got sick and I couldn't perform."

One of the best experiences of my life was when I had the opportunity to dance in London in a *pas de deux*. Amazing. A new *Nutcracker* in front of Tamara Rojo, the English National Ballet Artistic Director and Lead Principal Dancer. Then suddenly I got sick the week before and I couldn't perform.

There are good things and bad things in life. I think life is like that for everyone. You need to face the negative things to resolve them. Resolving them is part of life. We have to face these problems.

I study professional ballet at the English National Ballet School. It's difficult because I have a lot of good experiences but also bad experiences. When I danced in my first ballet, *Swan Lake*, I had the opportunity to learn the principal role. Unfortunately, the more you push yourself, the more you can be injured. I hurt my ankle, and I didn't say anything, the week before the premiere in London. I kept dancing and made it worse.

What I've learned from this is that when you are injured you have to tell people. You have to be intelligent about this. I've learned it's more important to be healed than to be famous. In any job. The bad things that happen in life teach you more than the good things.

When things go wrong, I tell myself it could be worse, and it can always be worse. I lost the opportunity to dance in London, but I had only twisted my ankle, so it took just one month to get better. I could have broken my leg. You can't dwell on losing an opportunity to dance. You have to think, 'What's best for me – to dance in one month or to be even more hurt than I am?' I have to think instead about how privileged I am to be in London and considered for a soloist position. It's a different way of looking at life, knowing your mind, being passionate about what you do, but also being a realist.

My dance career started thanks to one of my sisters because she was learning rhythmic gymnastics and I tried to copy the moves she was making. She would go to a sports centre and I went to see her and saw how she turned and twirled, and I liked it. At home my whole family were always dancing and loving music.

One day my parents said to me, 'You have to have a hobby.' I was 9 and I liked karate, so they said I could do karate. I thought music and dance were stupid because they were girlie, so I said I'd do karate because it was more masculine. I knew people could be mean if you were a boy and said you were a dancer. I made the wrong decision and didn't like it.

I decided very late to audition for the ballet school in my city. I turned up and everyone else was wearing ballet shoes and leotards. I had a tee-shirt and socks. I didn't know anything about dance. The jury put some pop music on for me in the final audition and, even though I was shy, I copied the moves and turns I'd seen my sister make in rhythmic gymnastics.

The school took me on, but most of the boys left because they were receiving bullying comments at school. 'You have to be gay to dance.' 'Dancing's for girls.' I think the others were being nasty because they hadn't had a break.

The first year was really good and then I started the second year and I had the opportunity to open a show with a girl in front of the whole ballet. After that performance I was put straight up to the third year. I was happy, but there is a lot of jealousy in dance, with other kids asking, 'Why are you here? Why did you miss a year?'

I'm not a jealous person. I try to help others. I like to be inspired by other people, see what they do and use that to improve what I do. I'm polite but many people aren't like that.

Ultimately, I would like to reach the top in the English National Ballet, but I also have to understand that it can be difficult to achieve your dreams. If you want to, you have to work; if you don't achieve it, you have to accept that you will still have a good life. These are normal experiences, learning to accept the negatives and the positives too. A bad experience can be good for you and teach you so much – far more than something positive. If you can't be Baryshnikov, you can still dance in a small theatre and be the best you can be and be happy with that. I have had some teachers who have been very hard on me, who didn't think I would achieve, but I have two loving parents and a very beautiful family. I am lucky.

I say to all teenagers: be yourself. If you want to do something, do it. You must love your own life. You can't do things for someone else. You'll find some rocks in your way, but you can use these to build your own wall. If you love someone and they don't love you, the world will still be turning. Try to achieve what you want and be the best you can. If you don't try, you will never know what you can do.

When I was dancing in Spain, I was in a competition and so was my friend. He was in the top team and I wasn't, which was frustrating. We both danced, and first prize went to my friend.

Then suddenly they announced, 'We have another prize, a special award from the jury,' and that was for me. So sometimes you can lose and you can win. And whatever happens, you'll still know more than you did before.

I believe that any time is a good time to fight for your dreams because it is never too late to try, but when we are young we have more motivation to face changes in our lives. We must be realistic and know we can't always fulfil our dreams, but it's so important to try to do what we want and what we dream.

HECTOR

@hectorvaloriaa

> "Any time is a good time to fight for your dreams because it is never too late to try, but when we are young we have more motivation to face changes in our lives."

YAMIKANI,

18, Lilongwe, Malawi

"The death of my mother resurrected the fighter in me. I told myself that I was going to work hard and reach the top. I will never be a failure."

My parents' divorce affected me badly as a child. I wanted to live with them both and felt divided in two. At times I wished I had never been born, it was so hard leaving my dad. I lived with my mother and my mother was also keeping her relatives as well, so I became part of an extended family living in poverty. I felt all the doors of opportunity had been closed behind me. My dreams had been broken.

Still I looked up to my mother. I remember how difficult it was for her to provide for the family. She kept on trying. She worked so hard. Then, when I was 8, she decided the best way for her to support us was to go to South Africa and get a job. The last thing I remember about her was her leaving in tears.

While she was out there, the worst thing happened. She died. I was 10 and I never saw her again. I find it difficult to believe that she has gone. We knew she was sick, but the doctors said she wasn't allowed anyone to tend to her. To them, there was nothing they could do to help save her life because she wasn't a citizen of the country and had no right to health care. We were unable to bring her body back home and they buried her just like that. So painful.

After her death, life was hard. I went to live with my dad who had remarried. My stepmother wasn't nice. She made it clear I was not her blood and made my life total hell. The peace of mind that I needed, even to walk with confidence in the streets, had gone.

Then I was so lucky because my aunt came and took me to live with her. She is so good; she is always there for me. Sometimes I miss Mum; sometimes I tell myself that it's OK because I have my auntie. It's OK.

Certainly the death of my mother has resurrected the fighter in me. These experiences, they motivated me. I told myself that I was going to work hard and reach the top. I will never be a failure. It took me time to realize that I can be the best only if I have an inner belief in myself. I began to resuscitate all my shattered dreams.

I have told myself that poverty is something I don't want my children to go through. I work hard now for the sake of the children I will have. I worked hard with determination, achieved good grades at school and I now have a place at the Public University of Malawi.

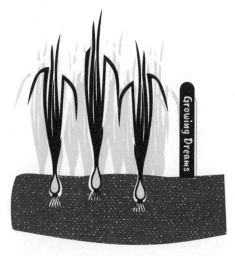

I am studying business studies and that will help me learn how to raise capital and develop other skills that I need. I want to run a farm as a business. I want to grow vegetables and keep animals. I want to be someone who can depend on herself. My early experience has taught me how important this is. My story will not be wiped out by failure but defined by hard work and determination.

Teenage years are a good time to make changes within myself and my community because at this age I know what I want. I know what is good and bad, and I have the energy and time to participate in community development before I am too busy with motherhood and other responsibilities.

Financial problems can be a challenge; even being a girl can be a challenge; but I just want to be the best of me. I believe in myself and I want to show everyone what I'm capable of doing. I want Dad to regret leaving me. I want to show him I will be a good woman and a great woman; a role model for other girls.

At the moment I am a role model by being a young Guiding leader. I want to be an agent of change for younger girls. I know now that problems are not there to push me down but to make me stronger, and I tell them the same.

I teach the younger girls how to reuse and recycle things. I teach them how to make their own sanitary pads from cotton and other material. They know how important it is to learn this skill and they are very pleased when I show them. Before this they just used their clothes when they had their periods and washed them out after school. And before they did this they weren't able to go to school when they had their period, and they missed out on their education.

I tell the girls you have to believe because the world is waiting for you to stand up and give it your all. Look at yourself in the mirror and love the girl you see.

YAMIKANI

f Malawi Girl Guides
  Association (MAGGA)

🐦 @GirlGuidesMw

www www.magga.org

> "Teenage years are a good time to make changes within myself and my community because at this age I know what I want."

CAMERON,

17, Harrogate, England

"Because I had cerebral palsy I was stuck on the bench at football and left out of matches. So I set up my own team, Adversity United."

I started getting into football in primary school when I was 6, when all my friends were playing. I loved it – I might be obsessed! At 10 I joined my local football club, but because I have cerebral palsy I didn't get on well there.

Cerebral palsy affects my left side, so when I was very young, I crawled a bit funny, dragging a hand and leg behind. I didn't learn to walk until later than the other kids.

Through life, my arm and leg improved. A lot of things have helped. I've done physio and I think playing football in my back garden was good for me, as was an Indonesian martial art called Silat. I visited a centre to do exercises to improve my mobility and wore splints for my arm and leg. When I was younger, a lot of people pointed them out – it's not your everyday thing to see. I was a bit different, but I wasn't too bothered. I knew they were there to help me and I just got used to them. This was thanks to my parents who said, 'You need to wear these splints,' and at that age you do what your parents tell you.

At primary school I really enjoyed playing football with my friends. It was when I joined the team that people could see I wasn't as good as other kids. I wasn't as mobile as the other players as I could only properly move on one side.

Because of this I was stuck on the bench and left out of matches. I could hear the coach and the players pointing out that I wasn't very good. I think people have come a long way since, but then it wasn't a very nice environment.

This mainly affected me because football is such a passion for me. It was a weird experience and boring sitting on the bench for every game on a Sunday and it did upset me. It was a waste of my time and a waste of my parents' time. I knew I wasn't ever going to have any chance of improving as I only ever got to play when there weren't enough players. I never started a game. Football was everything I thought about all week, but I felt that I had no choice but to leave.

Instead of football, I concentrated on my martial art. I felt included there and it gave me opportunities to grow. I started teaching the younger ages. I got my junior black belt when I was 13/14; then went on to do my adult black belt when I was 15. I started teaching people of all ages.

I've supported Manchester United since I was young as my mum's side of the family are from there. I still watched football on TV and went to a few matches, but I love football so this didn't feel like enough for me. I had started off playing in the garden, had gone to a team, and here I was back playing in the garden. I didn't have any opportunity to progress and this upset me.

Then a great thing happened. When I was 15, someone came to my school to teach us wheelchair basketball and he told me about cerebral palsy football, so I contacted them.

I was so excited at the thought of playing football for a team again. The manager of the Yorkshire Cerebral Palsy Squad asked me to go along to a disability centre in York and after two sessions I was invited to trial for the squad. I was buzzing at the thought that I could play for a team, not just in my back garden.

I've now been playing for them for three seasons, usually as a winger. I think it's built in me to play football. I don't know where I get it from.

By the end of the first season I had trials for the England Cerebral Palsy Development Squad. I didn't think I would ever be playing for my country because of my difficulties, but this allowed me to hope I would one day. Now in the last few months I've been asked to join the England Cerebral Palsy Under 21s for the rest of the season. I have my first camp this weekend. I've found my pathway and I've never looked back.

This has helped to improve my life, not just my football. It has given me confidence. I have found that the teamwork and the communication you need to do well have really helped me.

When I was 16 in September last year, I set up my own team, Adversity United. I decided to follow my dream of becoming a football coach.

At Adversity United we accept everyone who has a disability. It's all about inclusion – involving people who may not have access to mainstream football. It's about having fun and encouraging others. That's why I created it – and to give something back that wasn't there for me. We now have 15 players, all primary age, and I'm looking to get a few more for next season. We have such a good connection. The players and the families that surround them are brilliant.

Some of the kids haven't played football before, so I thought it might be upsetting to throw them into a full match. Instead, we are looking to do some friendlies this season, so they can have the opportunity to find out what that's like.

I'd like to go on to include teenagers. I have schoolwork to do as well, but I'm spending as much time on this as I can – and it looks like it might turn into my career.

From everything I've learned, I think the most important thing about any of this is to build confidence, to start to stretch yourself in what you can do, believe you can do something and go on and do it. I went to a lot of meetings with sponsors and that was well outside my comfort zone – an absolute stretch for me. You just have to believe in yourself.

I soon realized I got such a buzz out of going to the meetings that I thought, 'What else can I do?' At first, I wasn't used to this but now it's so natural and I feel I can achieve so many things. We have sponsors on our kits. The local newspaper and radio station are supporting us. The local football club gave us balls and bibs. My parents have done the Leeds half marathon to help us raise money; my dad's done a parachute jump and we are all doing the Tough Mudder obstacle course. I'm still not as good as everyone else in activities; I'm different to people you see on a day-to-day basis; but I have really good friends and a really good family.

I recently found out that I have been shortlisted for the National Diversity Awards, nominated by more than 300 people. It's great to get that kind of public acknowledgement.

In the past I have had moments when I've got upset, angry or frustrated, like when my friends were playing in the team I felt excluded from – that was quite difficult. It doesn't happen too much now. I'm so enjoying being who I am; I have got to a good point.

I have learned that the key for all of us is just be positive and believe that you can do things you want to do, even if it's a small thing. I started off small and worked my way up and built up to where I am now. It was difficult at the start and I haven't always been the most positive. But if there's a new skill you want to master, believe in yourself that you can do it, then stretch yourself to a harder challenge. Go from there. Small incremental achievements make all the difference.

CAMERON

🅕 Adversity United

🅧 @AdversityUnited

🅞 @adversityunited

"If there's a new skill you want to master, believe in yourself that you can do it, then stretch yourself to a harder challenge... Small incremental achievements make all the difference."

XANTHE,

19, London, England

"Grief has taught me that life is about happy memories. There is something life enhancing about opening up about death and talking about it."

Until I was 5 I had a very normal nuclear, suburban family with my mum, dad and two brothers. We had a lovely home. We would go on great family holidays. All very peaceful.

When I was 5, my mum was expecting my little sister. They found out during the pregnancy that she was going to be born with Down's syndrome, but when she was born they found out she also had Costello syndrome, a rare genetic disease affecting only 200 people in the world. This brought a lot of complications to the digestive system and increased her chance of developing cancer. It also meant she wouldn't have enough growth hormones and would have very distinctive features.

None of this got in the way of my excitement about having a little sister. I was over the moon for it, even though Daisy spent the first year of her life in hospital. The long hospital stay meant my mum and dad were travelling back and forth, leaving me and my older brother to be independent. We had that back-and-forth rhythm for most of Daisy's life. When she was born, I didn't quite click that she wouldn't grow up to be an able-bodied sister. I enjoyed playing dressing up with her and making tea parties, but I had to get used to the way that having a sister would bring many difficulties.

We were taught from a young age that Daisy's disabilities meant that it was unlikely that she would grow up to be an adult. We tried to do as much as we could with her, to have as many happy memories as possible in the short time we had.

For me, after the age of 5, it was always difficult to pretend that life was normal. The years going to Great Ormond Street Hospital to see my sister were the same years my friends were going on holiday. We lived in an entirely different world.

What's strange is that while our family was trying to be as normal as possible, we had more and more difficult things to deal with. My older brother, Theo, had a lot of behaviour issues when he was a teenager, getting into trouble at school. He was diagnosed with Asperger's. Then Jules, my younger brother, was diagnosed with pathological demand avoidance (PDA), a form of autism. The two of them are always locking horns.

I think I felt quite irritated by this. I didn't understand why they would get on each other's nerves so much – why they just couldn't behave like normal brothers, like my friends' brothers seemed to be, giving each other a hug. They both seemed to find it impossible ever to apologize and say they were wrong. Even on holiday, they would get on each other's nerves, pushing each other's buttons. This made the stress of dealing with Daisy much worse.

Then, in 2014, Dad was diagnosed with cancer. He had a year of treatment. We were very lucky we had that extra year to spend with him. In most cases of his type of cancer, you would have a few months or weeks.

He passed in December 2015, two weeks before Christmas, a huge stress on Daisy who died a year later when she was 12. We think Dad's death contributed to her deteriorating. Gradually, what had been looking like a very normal family had turned into a very different one.

Things are very different since Dad and Daisy passed away. It's still chaotic with the boys, busy and stressful, but there has been so much loss.

I had been in denial that Dad was terminally ill. Our outlook around Daisy had been very positive. We always knew we wanted to make the most of what time we had with her. With Dad we went to Glastonbury, we went out for dinner; we were never stingy – never saving anything for a rainy day. We didn't know how much time he had left. Because I was in denial about the severity of Dad's illness, that made it a lot more difficult when he died. With Daisy, I was prepared; that was my mindset. The grieving process had already begun and I knew what was going to come.

When Dad died, we visited him at the funeral home and we said our last goodbyes. With Daisy, we were very fortunate in that we could bring her body home from Great Ormond Street. She was at home and at peace. We took her lines out and took away all the medical accessories. Because she was on a cold mattress to preserve her body, we could sit with her whenever we wanted, put flowers in her hair, talk to her and play her favourite music. People from her school could say their goodbyes, as well as her nurses and carers. That was really great for getting closure for me. It showed me how much of an impact she'd had on people's lives. It gave me such a positive outlook on grief. Her life was a positive one. She'd had a big effect on others, despite her young age.

Grief has taught me that life is about happy memories. There is something life-enhancing about opening up about death and talking about it, not being too closed off, even making jokes about it. Being light-hearted keeps the communication channels open and allows people to talk about what they've been through. I find most people are bottled up and don't know whether to talk to me about it. It's important to me that they don't see me as closed off and they don't close off to me. I want to keep talking, even when it's tough. If people shut down because they don't know what to say, I feel cut off from the group. So I have to take control of what has happened to the family and get what I want from the conversations.

People say 'you are so brave' or 'so inspirational'. I reject that. That makes me feel like a martyr or a saint. I wasn't chosen for this to happen to me; it could have happened to anyone. Everyone else will go through difficult things in their lives, maybe different situations, maybe going through them in a different way. I try to be positive, open and relaxed about my story.

My best friend of more than six years has been through this, alongside me. She was here when everything happened. One thing I really appreciate about her is that she sees me as being positive and a strong person. She knows sometimes I will have down days and weaknesses. She knows these things will always affect me emotionally. She also sees me as open. It's so important to be open – this allows another person to support you.

As I have matured, it's easier to put what's happened into terms for people to cope with. I have days when I feel down about my life, but it has made me who I am. It has allowed me to mature as a person and given me emotional development. It's taught me to have attitude and be outspoken. It's given me an emotional experience around disability and this has made me a lot more empathetic to global issues.

The days I am depressed are balanced out with the emotional maturity. By default, I hope I'm teaching other people about the positive side you can always gain and use from what has happened.

I am showing that you can take what has happened and, rather than feeling bad about it, use it to your advantage. These things have happened to me, but I'm in a much better place. I'm living a better life. I have taken my lemons and turned them into lemonade.

XANTHE

 @xanimmo

> "You can take what has happened and, rather than feeling bad about it, use it to your advantage."

3...

FINDING
MY VOICE

JOSIE,

16, California, USA

"Everyone's scared to begin with, but we can all make changes if we try. Each time we make a stand, more people will stand up with us."

One of the issues in our school is about what we wear. Every time the girls wear ripped jeans, we get stopped in the corridors and dress-coded. When we wear shorts in the summer, we are dress-coded. Boys wear ripped jeans and shorts and they don't get stopped. A group of us girls are planning a petition to make a change to the dress code for the girls.

In the journalism class we asked questions to the administration about this. We said, 'What about our education? Does it not matter if we can't go to class because we've been dress-coded?' Someone at the school said girls should know what they look good in, which was so demeaning. It's about what we want to wear – it shouldn't matter to anyone else.

What helps us fight these issues are the monthly meetings we have with Girls Learn International, an organization of young feminists in high schools. We talk about how we can raise awareness in our schools. I've found that if you take the first step, others will follow. Everyone's scared to begin with, but we can all make changes if we try. Each time we make a stand, more people will stand up with us.

A lot of the time what we're doing is getting other people to realize what's happening. With the ripped jeans thing, the girls didn't realize the boys weren't getting stopped. They were just thinking, 'It's school. It's what happens.' Now they know this is happening right now, and we are allowing it to happen.

Something one of the girls at school is thinking of changing is in the bathrooms. She is looking to adopt the 'pad project' she heard about in another school. This is a great idea to help girls who can't afford sanitary protection or who have forgotten theirs, which can be a real embarrassment. Girls would leave a new pad behind once they have used the bathroom and a girl could take one if they needed it. Apparently, this works really well.

Bringing awareness and finding support helps you to make change where you want it. I think that this is definitely one of the things that has made me more powerful. So many things that I see are demeaning to me and the people I love. Self-belief is very important. I know many people think teenagers are just kids, but we are the future and we need to start showing what we want.

In my experience, I think the negative responses to what we are doing come from our Latino community. The men are put first and that mindset that's been there for centuries is still continuing.

My dad doesn't believe in feminism because of the machismo in our culture. I still continue doing what I believe is right and makes a difference. It's definitely a struggle with him and it has been challenging, but I know that small victories will help him change.

I have done dancing, cheerleading – what my dad wanted for me as a girl. Now I'm taking on more challenges at school, he's saying, 'Go to dance practice.' I say, 'I can do anything I want.' I have a strong support system. I come from a family of five girls, and just one little brother who is still a baby. So Dad's outnumbered! He needs to help us stand up for ourselves. I think he's slowly coming to realize that. I did an internship in a law firm and saw that the women there were secretaries: not attorneys, not senior associates, not partners. We need to make these changes.

Now is a good time for teenagers to express what we want. For me, I think getting into journalism with a strong set of beliefs

means I would be able to express myself and make that happen
and that's what I want to do. I am part of an organization called
Global Girl Media. With them, I've just created a documentary
about mental illness in the people of color community. I wanted to
destigmatize it as we know how hard it is to get help.

We found a lot of statistics which show the very limited access
to services and that, because of our customs and beliefs, none of
our family and friends talked about this.

Through Girls Learn International I am going to attend the UN
Women's Commission in New York with a scholarship they gave
me. We are going to be the voice for teenage women. We will draw
up a list of some of the changes we want to see in the world. I'm
looking forward to being with other teenage activists. I think what
I want to do is to realize what has affected me and then see what
others think the problems are. I see how teens are rising up and
I'm going to help them make changes. We can come together and
be stronger.

Once you start identifying the problems and noticing what's
happening around you, there's a fire inside you that gets brighter
and brighter. We will put out that fire only by making change.

JOSIE

@ @justxjosie

> "Many people
> think teenagers
> are just kids, but
> we care about the
> future and we need
> to start showing
> what we want."

ZAINAB,

17, Nelson, Lancashire, England

"I've stopped being a rebel and I came back into school as a youth worker to help young kids, putting them on the right track."

I had always been gobby. I was always a rebel. I would argue with my classmates and the teachers for no reason. I was a pain. Then I started hanging around with the wrong crowd and taking the wrong path. There was a lot of bad influence.

Then the truth hit me. I was isolated. I was the class clown and being an idiot, and it wasn't going to get me anywhere. I had this anxiety that was hurting me mentally and physically. I talked to the youth worker at school and he said to me, 'You yell at the teachers. You are the Queen Bee. Why don't you use your loud voice and aggression for something good?' He said there was good in me and why didn't I do something with that. I listened to him and moved away from those friends. I wasn't the idiot any more. I turned into the girl people could go to for help. I became part of the youth committee. Whenever people had problems, they would speak to us and we addressed our concerns to the teachers.

I changed from the girl I used to be. It was hard to get out of the mindset of messing about. I still have that rebel side to me, but things are different now. One younger girl at school said the other day, 'Zainab inspires me. I heard from teachers how bad you used to be. You had the confidence to change.' It made me cry to think what I've done has made a difference. Adults think teenagers are useless, always on social media, but some of us out there really can make a difference to the world. We need our voices to be heard.

Regret is the worst pain. If you don't want to have pain and guilt in your life, then don't do the things that will cause these emotions. This behaviour can cost you a lot. You may be entertaining your friends, but at the end of the day your friends will walk away with the GCSEs and you'll have none and then you'll be the true clown.

I have new friends now. I'm no longer a sheep following others; I'm the shepherd. I'm my own person. It's way better.

One thing I'm really proud of is a project I did on World War One. I am from Asian heritage and I never knew how Asia contributed to World War One. I didn't know if anyone in my family had contributed. Our group went to Belgium, France, Brighton and London to investigate.

We found out in Brighton that many Indian troops stayed there. They were given a separate area to cook their food. There were different areas for the Muslims and Hindus to pray in. People took care of them. I tried to find if there were records about my granddad, but the records of the ordinary soldiers were lost when the partition between India and Pakistan happened.

After we did this research, our group was invited to a remembrance festival. I made a speech at the Royal Albert Hall in front of the Queen, which was shown on TV, talking about how remembrance means so much to me as an individual. I said we should all embrace it – not just white people. I had three panic attacks during the rehearsal; I was so stressed I would get it wrong. Then when I spoke, everyone was clapping. I asked my teacher if the Queen was looking at me. People came up to me and said, 'How can you have the confidence to speak like that with people watching you on telly?'

I want to get somewhere where my voice is heard so I'm thinking of going into journalism or politics. I want to use my voice in a positive way. I want to influence all young people who think they have no say. I've left school now, but I come back in as a youth worker and help young kids, putting them on the right track.

Many come from backgrounds where they mess about; they've decided they're not going to take school seriously. It's easy for me to work with them because I was like that. Sometimes teachers don't understand them, but it's easy for me to get through to them because I've come from that place myself.

I'm the type of person now who loves people and loves nature. If I see suffering, I have to help. It's our job to look after each other. I want to make sure the right things are said, the right voices are out there.

Mum was crying with pride when she saw me on TV. I was wearing my scarf as well as my school uniform. When I started changing, she said, 'Are you OK? I thought you would always be this idiot.' She says I'll go so far in life. My little brother has also picked himself up and is on right path, and he says I'm his inspiration. Some people might criticize and say I'm a teacher's pet but I'm not going to let someone's five seconds ruin my entire day. It's never once stopped me. If it's going to benefit me, I'll do it.

ZAINAB

"Adults think teenagers are useless, always on social media, but some of us out there really can make a difference to the world. We need our voices to be heard."

HANNAH,

19, Preston, England

"I struggled with being shy and speaking out but I gave a talk to a United Nations conference of 500 people."

I was always a shy child. I have always struggled with making friends and speaking out. I didn't even like answering questions in class.

I have coeliac disease and my pituitary gland stopped functioning properly when I was younger. I became underweight and my health conditions became so serious that they kept me out of school for four years when I was in my teens. I started secondary school in September and a few months later I couldn't go anymore.

While I was at home and poorly, I felt forgotten and left out. I felt it was my fault that I was ill and that I wasn't able to go to school. It may sound daft to think that, but you start to go through these thought processes.

I had gone up to high school with a group of friends from primary. By the time I went back when I was 15, I had lost that friendship group. They had moved on. That was so hard and really knocked my confidence. My old friends were into sports and were in different clubs which I couldn't be part of because of my health. They were going off to matches and I felt very isolated.

Only in the last couple of years have I felt comfortable to talk about how painful this was. I was bitter about it then, but now I'm not because it's shaped me into the person I am.

My ill health means that I am someone who was close to not being here anymore. This means I see things in a different way. I'm much more confident and resilient than if I hadn't been through everything I've been through.

I know that you only live once and I am determined to make the most of my life. In time I formed a new friendship group, which gave me so much confidence. So has being a Brownie leader. I joined the Brownies when I was 7; then joined the Guides when

I was well enough, when I was 15. At that time I went back to the Brownie unit to volunteer and help others. This gave me something else to focus on and a different set of skills to build. It was incredibly rewarding to give something back and to help others. I also went to Rangers, which has an older age range, and made friends there – a massive boost for me.

I love everything to do with Guides and happened to see the opportunity on Twitter to be part of a delegation to a huge United Nations conference in New York on gender equality and women's rights. The role was to represent and speak out for young women and girls all across the world. I have always been interested in human rights and feminism, so I jumped at the chance to take part. I thought it sounded amazing. I struggled with the application form but I wrote the best answers I could. I thought even if I didn't get chosen, I have done my best. Then I had a phone call telling me I had got through to the phone interview stage. Then I heard I had been selected to represent the UK, to join another representative from Scotland and one from Ireland.

I ran around the house in excitement. I was over the moon. Then a few days later I suddenly thought, 'I have got to do this.' The panic set in. I did some webinars and training on public speaking and everything I needed to know about women's rights, and did some more research and concluded that it wasn't going to be too bad.

On my way to New York I was excited. Then when I got there, there was more training. I remember on the first day of training, the World Association of Girl Guides' staff were grilling us to get information out of us to practise what it would be like at the conference. All of a sudden, I just burst into tears. It was so intense. My brain felt so slow, trying to take all the information in. I thought, 'I'm here. I can't turn around and go. I'm stuck in a corner.' I didn't feel I could do it. Then they told me not to cry and reassured me. They said they had seen something in me or they wouldn't have chosen me to be there.

I had found out when I arrived that my speech was going to be the first one at the conference. I would be talking in front of representatives from different charities and NGOs from all over the world. I would be on a panel in front of 500 people. It was very scary. I had a lot of help from the staff, and what was really amazing was that the other girls there who I had only just met felt like sisters. We had such a strong bond. It was overwhelming knowing that there was this group of people rooting for me, really wanting me to succeed. I took this in at a deep level. Having not been accepted into the group at school, I now felt, 'Wow. I am accepted.' There are no words to describe the level of confidence this gave me in myself.

I was so nervous, but my speech went well. It went really well. I talked about my life experience and how being a guide helped me. The other girls had helped me to prepare and a lot of Guides came along to watch my speech. I kept my focus on them and ignored everyone else and my confidence shot up through the roof.

What was really sweet was that the girl from Scotland and I went to a debrief organized by the UK government. They had been told about the speech I had given that day and wanted to hear more about it. Afterwards everyone clapped. Even Jess Phillips, an MP, burst into tears and talked to me afterwards to thank me for sharing my story and told me I was very brave.

My life so far has taught me that it's really important to be confident in who you are. A lot of the time there's a lot of pressure to fit in and be like everyone else and look a certain way. It's a challenge and I don't think I have got there fully, but my goal is not to worry about what other people think. Never be afraid to go for something and see how you get on.

Why we have that pressure is down to a mixture of things.

Social media is a massive one, but also magazines, newspapers, adverts, films, TV. There's a lot of pressure on boys as well.

There's a lot of pressure to be academic, to go from high school to college and get a top career. There's not much emphasis on other routes. It's hard for me to catch up because I missed so much school. Very, very tough. I did well in my GCSEs because I pushed myself. Afterwards I thought, 'I'm fine now,' but I started A levels and burnt myself out. I had to come out of them because I couldn't cope. Since then, I've done odd jobs and I'm still trying to decide what I want to do, but I know I want to do something that helps other people or helps society in a bigger way. I feel I have something that will allow me to give back to the world or give back to other people.

When I was helping out with the Brownies, seeing those shy 7-year-olds grow in confidence into adventurous 10-year-olds was very satisfying. I think that's what I want to do with my career – help shape someone else's life. I know as well as anyone that, when you need it, accepting help is so important.

I think it's important to be true to yourself. Follow your passions and give everything your best shot. Learning to be comfortable with who you are takes time and can be difficult. But getting to know who you are and accepting yourself while you're a teenager can really help you become a stronger person and help you live your best life.

HANNAH

@han_sandy30

> "It was overwhelming knowing that there was this group of people rooting for me, really wanting me to succeed."

HERAA,

20, Colorado, USA

"Losing everything I owned helped teach me to stand up for my community."

W **hen I was in 8th grade,* at home with my two-year-old sister, our house burnt down.**

Dad was at work and Mum was at the doctors. We ran out and saw the whole block on fire. The fire fighters said if we had waited 30 seconds longer, we wouldn't have made it. I called Dad and he called Mum. The fire could be seen from 20 miles away. We lost everything except for the cars because my parents were in them. We didn't have a certain kind of insurance, so for a while we were homeless.

I remember this feeling of hopelessness because I didn't feel I could do anything; I had no semblance of control. For that whole year I was struggling, dealing with depression and PTSD.

I had never been in a position where I didn't know where my next meal was coming from. I was used to a comfortable lifestyle, with my own room, living the American dream. I was a 13-year-old and obsessed with the things I owned. Then I had nothing. This experience taught me that material things may be nice, but they are not important. They give you nothing back.

I realized that when I am older and looking back at my life, I didn't want to think that all I had done was to accumulate things.

As I came to terms with what had happened and thought of the positives, I realized that as a family we became a lot closer after the fire. We were closer to our friends and the people around us. They supported us and looked after us, and I don't know how we will ever pay them back. Good things come out of bad. My sense of the importance of community had grown.

---

*   Ages 13–14.

I think this is one of the influences that brought me to campaigning. Then there was a build-up of a lot of things I heard and things that were said to me. There was an attack in London; there were a few attacks here that had been used to push a discriminatory agenda, around the time of the election in 2016. As all of this was happening, I saw that I lot of the rhetoric lacked intelligence and facts. One question I was asked at school was 'Why are Muslims so violent?' I could feel myself building up an argument, but I felt I wasn't getting a voice.

I went home so frustrated. I knew other attacks were happening, but these were not presented as 'terror attacks'. I thought I could send the girl who asked me that question a few links and tell her to Google the answer, but instead I started to research. I started to learn more about my own faith. Rejection of violence and war was one thing; refutation of the Isis theology was another. I started going down this big rabbit hole; I did this big Google vibe.

Altogether I put together a Google spreadsheet with a 712-page list of what Muslims condemn, from terrorism to discrimination against women to climate change. It took me three weeks of work. Eventually, I thought, 'I can make this a resource.' I did what any sane teenager did and tweeted what I had learned.

Overnight I had thousands and thousands of retweets – 15,000 retweets in 24 hours. I realized this is something that the public needs. We had been defending the Muslim community, but we didn't realize what the facts were.

I started to get a lot of messages about what I'd done. Then a web developer from Nigeria messaged me to say this would be great information to make into a website. I didn't notice his message and then I saw a second message from him that said, 'The website is 70 per cent ready!' He had set up the Muslims Condemn website and he is still running it now with his girlfriend, not wanting any publicity or money for it. I'm blown away by that.

What we had done was then picked up by the Bridge Initiative in Washington. They are also involved in breaking down misconceptions about Islam with factsheets and workshops. They had been working on these for some time. They had 600 examples and I had 6000. That's what happens when you're a student and you don't sleep! They said, 'Why don't we pool our resources?' So we did.

I received a lot of criticism for what I was doing. Some people said to me, 'If the Ku Klux Klan launches an attack and uses Christ as a justification, individual Christians are not held accountable. Christians wouldn't feel the need to do what you are doing.' But I felt it was important to show people that what they were thinking about Muslims wasn't true.

I get some hate messages once in a while, usually from accounts where all they do is hate on other people's accounts. I'm not too concerned. I wouldn't block anyone if they asked me a question, but if they come back calling me names, I'm not happy about that. My parents remind me, 'Don't get angry, don't respond in any way, nothing is forever deleted.'

Then the Yaqeen Institute invited me to give a lecture in front of 3000 Muslims. This put me in the running for the Muhammad Ali Confident Muslim Award. Somehow, I was selected as the winner. I got to go down to Dallas and have lunch with the daughters of

Malcolm X and Muhammad Ali. I felt so honored to be with them and it gave me passion to follow in their footsteps. What was amazing was that these two daughters were talking about their fathers as ordinary people, but they were the best of the ordinary. Rashida Ali was saying that her dad would never turn away from a fan. Once they were in a limo after a screening and someone started running after the car and he told the driver to stop even though he was tired and jet-lagged. He got out of the car and took a picture and did an autograph and talked to him one to one. He never thought himself above the people.

Malcolm X's daughter was so eloquent. I thought I would have to pull out a dictionary, she's so academic. She talked about her dad having made the effort to integrate them into every community: they would go to church, synagogue, Catholic school… This is the example we can learn from.

Everyone at the table was enraptured. These daughters reaffirmed my love and belief in these men. They reminded me that I was not the one bringing change. There was Malcolm X, there was Muhammad Ali. These are the people who were handing down legacies.

At college I am studying Molecular, Cellular and Developmental Biology with a minor in Linguistics. My parents are mainly concerned about my grades. I'm hoping to get into grad school and research bioinformatics, but I imagine that Muslims Condemn will be a huge part of my life. Starting the campaign was a pivotal moment for me. It made me realize we have the capacity to do a lot of good in the world and make a lot of change.

I want to make sure my intentions are sincere. I want to make sure I'm not doing this for attention, but because I truly care about the condition of the people.

Growing up in the digital world has enabled me to do what I have done. We are the generation able to achieve this. I have added a design tech certificate to my studies and in class we have talked about how tech is not evil; it's a tool and it's dependent on the user. The Parkland high school shooting has pushed teenagers into the spotlight, trying to push for change. Tech is their form of connection and it's a reality. I make the choice to use tech for good every day. Whether I get one like or a thousand likes, it's enough. We don't need to be Instagram stars known by the public; we just need to be ourselves and push for change where we feel it's needed. That's our job as young people.

HERAA

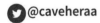 @caveheraa

Photograph of Heraa by Office of Diversity, Equity and Community, CU Boulder

> "I felt it was important to show people that what they were thinking about Muslims wasn't true."

WENDY,

18, California, USA

"I know that I can't change anything from my past, but I do have the power to shape my future."

In October 2017 *The New York Times* published the first story about sexual harassment claims against the film producer **Harvey Weinstein.** Many months after this story made headlines, it was still dominating the news channels. More and more actresses came forward as time went by. The hashtag that accompanied their stories was #MeToo.

I have lived through sexual assault and I can tell you there is nothing that I fear more than having to tell my story and facing the risk that people won't believe me. Telling my story wasn't easy the first time around, and it doesn't get any easier the third or fourth.

As more and more actresses came out from the shadows, something in me changed. I felt an empowerment that I hadn't felt before. I read article after article about why they decided to tell their stories. One thing that surprised me was that most of the time they didn't tell their story to help themselves, but to help other young actresses who are trying to climb up the ladder of fame. They wanted to warn them; to protect them. After *Time* magazine published its issue 'Person of the Year 2017: The Silence Breakers' as a tribute to these brave women, I realized I was witnessing history.

At the same time, a controversial Netflix show began airing called *13 Reasons Why*. It recounts the story of a 16-year-old girl named Hannah Baker who committed suicide as the result of abuse. A conversation started in schools surrounding the topics covered in the show. Once I heard my male classmates asking each other who in their right mind, in Hannah's situation, would not ask for help. It was as if they were blaming her.

I remember very clearly the moment I turned around and said something along the lines of 'Who in their right mind would rape anybody?'

After this, they chose their questions more carefully; they tried to place themselves in the shoes of the victim. This to me was a little victory in and of itself.

This small victory helped me understand why it was important for me to speak up, especially for those that aren't capable of sympathizing with victims of this horrendous act. As part of my treatment (I had to go through various psychologists to help me with the trauma), I went to 'talking groups' where I would hear different stories from women and men who were also enduring the trauma. This led me to want to talk to other people, on an individual basis, to help them endure their own troubles. Helping others was therapeutic to me and led me to believe that I can actually make change happen.

During the abuse I experienced, which was by an ex-boyfriend, I had felt both defenseless and responsible: as if it was my fault. I did not know what to do or who to tell. Telling my family didn't feel like an option, as I didn't know how they would react. My mother noticed that I was living in fear and she found a diary I had kept. She read about the depth of my feelings, that sometimes I felt suicidal, and placed me in the hands of psychologists who sent me to a psych ward. Here I reflected on what had happened and how I was going to cope with the aftermath of the assault.

When my case came to court, it took a lot of courage to give my testimony. My ex-boyfriend pleaded guilty but was given only community service and therapy, which felt like a slap in the face.

But what is powerful is that I can now write my story without trembling or shedding a tear. Sometimes I ask myself what I could've done to change the course of events, but then I shut up that part of my brain. I know that I can't change anything from my past, but I do have the power to shape my future. I am currently in uni and my dream is to get my bachelor's in Journalism. It'll be a long way to get there, but I'm up for the ride.

To anyone reading this, please heed the lesson I have learned. If you or a loved one is going through a similar situation to mine, don't hesitate to get help for yourself or for them. I've encountered people in my life, girls and boys, who tell me that they're in similar situations and that they don't know what to do. I usually steer them to a professional to get them help. Most of the time, I watch them come back to me and thank me for helping them, and I usually make them promise me never to put themselves in such danger ever again if they can help it. Throughout this process

YOU CAN CHANGE THE WORLD!

of getting help myself and for others, I've learned that most of the time victims don't ask for help because they're terrified and afraid of getting judged, but my message to you is please speak up; if not for you, then do it for somebody else. You can relieve yourself from a heavy weight. You can save the next victim.

WENDY

@ @wendyrhblogs

@ Wendy R. H.

"Helping others was therapeutic to me and led me to believe that I can actually make change happen."

MAYA,

19, Damascus,

Syria and

Birmingham, England

"My message to other refugees is that you do get bad times, but things will change if you have a little hope."

My family is from Damascus, one of the cities affected by the bombing of Syria. While we were there, it was getting really bad. Essentials like electricity, water and gas were not available most of the time. I had to change schools three times. My first school couldn't be accessed because of army surrounding the school most of the time; the second school was supposed to be safer but wasn't and my mum was getting worried about me. One time when I was 15, I was going to the third school, walking on my own, when I just heard these awful shocks and explosions. I didn't know where to go. I didn't have a phone. I just stood still. I didn't know what to do. The bombs were banging louder. I felt surrounded and that there was no way out.

Looking back, I still feel blessed that nothing happened to any of our family.

We were scared because we were living in a dangerous place, but we still had our home. I really wanted to carry on with my education, but my parents thought we had to leave and find a safer placed to carry out our lives normally. My dad managed to get us visas and we arrived here by aeroplane. Not many people know that this is possible. They think refugees have all arrived after walking through the jungle.

I had never thought about coming to the UK. It was only when my dad came here safely in 2014 that he told us it would be a safe place for all of us. He applied for a family reunion visa which took 15 months to be approved. Then we had to go to the embassy in Lebanon, travel to Turkey and stay there for a month before we left for the UK. On the way, in the aeroplane, I was really excited. I had never flown before, so I was nervous, but I started having these hopes of a school with my own locker, and a uniform. I thought we would live in a big calm neighbourhood and the neighbours would bring chocolate cake and have children a similar age to me and we would play together, just like you see in the movies.

We arrived in May and that was when my life forcibly changed. What shocks people most is that they expect that I struggled to reach here, then was suddenly happier when I arrived and had an easier life afterwards.

For me, the upset came once I arrived. I was 16 and I felt dislocated in new surroundings; it was a whole new life and environment. The language was new. I had learned bits and pieces in Syria, but I had to get used to the Birmingham accent. I knew I had to do GCSEs, and I expected I would find a school and enrol, blend in and get used to people. But one school said their school was too advanced; I needed somewhere more basic. The next gave me a sticky note with the address of the council. The next one never wrote back. I went to a college and didn't hear back from them either.

This was harsh. I wanted to have a normal life; I wanted a basic thing which was to get into school. I was so ready for more knowledge. Mum and Dad left every morning to go to college to learn English; my little brothers were at school. I was left at home with nothing to do, no education, no friends. Just left there. I was isolated and lonely. I cried about my friends in Syria and asked myself why I had left them and my life there. My future had always been my top priority and it was dripping away.

I found English difficult because no one was teaching me. I bought a book and started reading and started forcing myself to use English more than Arabic. I made sure that I didn't translate anything to Arabic; I just read it in English. I listened to songs and read the lyrics. Finally, I went up to a teacher at a college and asked them to trust me that I could do my GCSEs. They tested my English and I was given a place at college and I started interacting with people. That's when my English properly improved, but I can tell you that learning the difference between who and how is hard!

My uncle had arrived in the UK the dangerous way, going from Turkey to Greece by boat, then going across different countries until arriving safely at the UK. This meant that once he arrived he received more help from the government who gave him addresses of organizations who help refugees. He told me about a project run by The Children's Society.

I went along to the project and I was one of a few teenagers there who made a small speech, talking about the chance we'd been given. Rosanne from The Children's Society came up to me at the end and said, 'You sounded amazing. We would love it if you helped us help other children.' I thought my English must be improving!

I think it was Rosanne who helped me gain confidence again. She made me see that people here are friendly and they do accept others. She made me believe I could be someone in this country. I decided I wanted other children to feel this too. I started to give talks about how I came to the UK, the struggles we'd had. I would go to the project in Birmingham and we'd all cook a meal together, explore Birmingham together and feel our English improve together. This was so different from feeling isolated and lonely at home.

Eventually, I became a volunteer speaker with The Children's Society. My message was that if you struggle, it's important to know that it's going to get better. I told them about being rejected by three schools and a college. Other people started asking me to come and speak. I talked about my story and about how The Children's Society gave me hope. I felt amazing. I realized how essential it is that people feel welcome. I want to get rid of the stereotypes about refugees. I'm telling people, 'This is who we are, this is who we are trying to be. These are the problems we face but we really appreciate the help we are receiving.' My message to refugees and migrants is that you do get bad times, but things will change if you have a little hope.

Now I now feel welcomed into the country and into the education system. People everywhere are lovely and supportive. I feel lucky and surrounded by good people.

I do miss Syria and my people there and my friends, but now I'm a different person. I'm no longer trying to blend in. I'm now trying to stand out. I'm showing that everyone is remarkable in their own way.

Three days before my 18th birthday, I learned I was going to be given the Diana Legacy Award, set up in honour of Princess Diana. It was so funny because my mum had told me, when we were going to the UK, 'We are going to see Prince William, we are going to see Prince Harry.' We thought they would be walking around casually and we'd be bumping into them in the street! When I went to receive the award, I thought they weren't going to be there, but they were. Both were so lovely. We had a small chat; they knew about all our stories and I received my award from both of them. I can describe the feeling and the day by saying it was supercalifragilisticexpialidocious. The palace, the royalty and the people were all surreal. I never expected all of this. Their Royal Highnesses were so lovely, and they made sure to speak to each one of us. When coming up to receive my award, each one of them told me supportive and encouraging words – I call them royal secrets – then gave me the award and I went back to my seat. I cried when I first stepped to the stage – the lights, clapping, cameras and people all made it something unforgettable. I remember thinking, 'Dreams do come true.'

Being rewarded in this way made me feel my message was recognized. People do listen. I work for The Children's Society to bring hope and understanding about refugees, and it was amazing to be rewarded for something I never thought I would be rewarded for.

Funnily enough, ever since our journey to the UK, I have been fascinated by aeroplanes. I remember being scared at the beginning because of the bumps, but then began the calm journey to a new life and that made a real difference. I have decided I am going to university to study to be an aviation engineer. I will end up with a pilot's licence and one day it will be me flying people to different countries. Extraordinary. I definitely feel like I should take the most advantage of my teen years. I feel that teen's are known for their youth and energy. If you have compassion and belief in your cause, those qualities will help you to get things done.

I have definitely changed hugely during these times. Coming here as a 16-year-old young adult was a change at a crucial time: when we start defining ourselves in this life, when we try to set goals and count our achievements. Since turning 19, I feel like I still have a lot to learn; at the same time, I still have a lot to call out for. With the advantage of being young, we can be heard, we can be listened to and our opinions can be valued. We should embrace those opportunities. Teenage years are when we have energy and enough compassion to do something we believe in. With the power that we have, the sky's the limit.

MAYA

 @GhazalMia

 @ghazalmia

> "We can be heard, we can be listened to and our opinions can be valued. Teenage years are when we have energy and enough compassion to do something we believe in."

4. . . .

CHALLENGING WHAT OTHERS THINK

JONATAN,

22, Helsinki, Finland

"I thought I was uncool moving into a retirement home, but the older people taught me so much."

I went to live in a retirement house for a year and a half with about 100 older people when I was 19. It was an amazing experience. I heard about history and learned about life.

When I moved in at first, I thought in a teenager-y way that what I was doing was uncool. What was very strange was that my friends, and my friends' friends, felt exactly the opposite. They were always supportive. They'd say, 'It's amazing that you are doing this.' I realized very quickly that they were right.

Most of the residents had some family, but some of them didn't have anyone at all. Some were in their 70s and some almost 100. I was there as a friend and a helper. I brought them coffee and spent time with them. When I did this, I could see in their faces how happy they suddenly were, just from me being there.

I think they enjoyed my company because, besides the nurses, all around them were people of the same age. Having someone there who was younger made their surroundings more interesting. It gave them a different perspective. In retirement homes it can seem like older people have been put into boxes, closed off from the outside world. Having me and other young people there brought the world they were living in to life.

My neighbour, who was 86, and I became really close friends and remained friends until she passed away a year ago. I still have good memories of her. She was a really good friend to me. What's lovely is that, whenever I think of her, I have this picture in my mind of her smiling.

One of the men in the retirement house fought in the war, but when they talked about history, mostly it was about the cold war between Finland and Russia. Nowadays you don't hear about these things. We are a pretty neutral country, so it was eye-opening listening to these stories.

Something I was taught by the people in the home is how important it is never to give up on the things that you love. They told me how important it is to do work you love and love the work you do.

I am a pastry chef. When I was living with them, I was studying to do this and brought home what I'd made during the day to share with them. When I graduated, I celebrated with them and brought cakes and pastries I'd made at school. They were very happy about that!

I paid rent while I was staying there, but it was really, really cheap for Finland: €250 instead of €800. The rents here are really high, so one reason the project had been organized was to show how a different kind of living can work for young people.

The project I was part of was very successful. I was one of three teenagers living there and, after we moved away, others came in. I think the project helped bring to light the problems connected with getting older. I think it gave me a strong message that I should care for elderly people and I should be more helpful to them.

When I was a boy, I was with my grandmother a lot and helped her whenever I could. After I left the retirement home, I started helping older people if I saw that they needed help: in the supermarket, in the street, anywhere I noticed that a helping hand might be welcome. It's these little things that make the heart warm. It brings something special to my life too. Little things can make such a difference.

To me now, it's unthinkable that anyone would think older people are 'just older'. I think their experience in life is much more valuable than the things that have developed now, such as technology. My friends there helped give me life lessons.

At work I bring joy into people's lives by making pastries. I think that is reflected in who I am. I sometimes sneak into the stores that sell my baking and see people buying the cakes and pastries and how happy it makes them. It makes me happy to see that and reminds me how happy it made the people in the retirement house too.

Back then I wasn't in a relationship. I think the way I changed by living there shows up in the relationships I have now with my boyfriend and my family. I have become a more caring person. I really do care. I want to help people.

I recommend that other teenagers should try this, or anything to do with helping people. If you have a neighbour who's elderly or anyone from the street who might need help, you can go and ask if they need help or if they'd like to talk, because a lot of them are really lonely. Some might not have been in touch with other people apart from nurses for years. I think we need to respect them and respect history. We are here because they are here and that's so important. I hope that other teenagers and young people will open their eyes and open their hearts to elderly people.

JONATAN

"It can seem like older people have been put into boxes, closed off from the outside world. Having me and other young people there brought the world they were living in to life."

LIAM,

17, Waroona,

Western Australia

"It's easy to be judgemental. I've learnt to be more open-minded. You never know what someone is going through."

I have just been lucky enough to take part in two weeks of exploring one of the United States' most beautiful protected lands, Shenandoah National Park. I was part of a scholarship program to encourage young people from different countries to become environmental leaders, wanting to make a difference.

The thing is that even now I'm back I don't consider myself to be a massive greenie. I'm not obsessed with the environment, though the trip has definitely made me think more about it and about climate change.

Instead, what I learned on the trip was largely about myself; and what I learned was life-changing.

The Nature Bridge Alcoa Scholars program recruits young people from many different countries and for two weeks we were like a family. We were with instructors who treated us like friends.

While I was there, it was the first anniversary of one of my best mates, Sam, who took his own life. The support I received from the others was one of the nicest things I have ever had done to me. No joke, I will remember that for the rest of my life.

For those two weeks I spent my time getting to know different people and I learned about what life is like for them, how their cultures are so different from Australia's. It was a big lesson to me that some things that we would be critical of here are not criticized in other places in the world. For example, over here it's considered weird if you like or read *Harry Potter*, for instance. In some countries, if you don't like *Harry Potter*, you are considered out of the normal.

This was my first lesson that Australia can be really judgemental. It got me thinking that people are not the same everywhere you go. I found that very interesting. What I learned definitely impacted on the way I am as a person. It has made a big difference to how I am in the world, the way I think of people and how people are different. Before the trip I would never have obviously judged some of the others but, internally, I would have thought of them as different to me. Now I think of them in a different light. Once I got to know them, they were all legends.

The others were saying that what they were hearing from me made them feel that Australia was a very judgemental place. Now I think that's true and I would love to do something, as small as it might be, to change that.

My friend who died seemed to me to be the happiest person. He always put himself before others. His death hit me pretty hard. In the area I live in, the suicide rate is huge, and now I wonder if that's something to do with how much people judge each other.

I wonder if people focus too much on how they come across, or if they are just trying to be the same as everyone else, trying to fit in. If they don't fit in, then people won't talk about this outwardly, but they will chuck them into a different group inside their head. Because they do something different, they will be automatically thought of as different. This might include kids playing chess, or card games with dragons on. These aren't things I find interesting, but now I think of people who do – good on them for being themselves.

Just the other day I was picked up with my girlfriend by her friend, who's African. The friend had to sit between us in the car, just because that's her culture. It would have been disrespectful for us to sit together. In her culture they see things differently. I wouldn't have noticed that before.

I'm more open-minded now about other people. If I hear someone saying something to someone now that they shouldn't be saying, I will tell them they shouldn't be saying it. I hope by doing this I can influence other people.

I'm not saying people here are bullying. I think a lot of us say things that we don't mean to be hurtful, that can be hurtful. Some comment or action can send someone over the edge. It doesn't matter how small what we say or do is. Saying something to someone can turn a small issue into something that's pretty big.

After Sam died, everyone was saying, 'I'm here for everyone.' People were talking about and writing about suicide and depression for many months, but it all died down and many people started to slowly forget. Don't be that person who forgets. Make a difference to the lives of others and be there for people because you never know what someone is going through.

Having been given the opportunity I have been given at such a young age, it has given me a different outlook on life. I'm already communicating more with all different types of people. Maybe the teen years are the years we can learn easily. We don't have the responsibilities that we will have when we're an adult, so we can make the most of opportunities while we're young. You don't have to go on a trip to the other side of the world. Ask someone if they are OK. Go out of your way to make a difference because you really can. It can change a life.

Life is short. We are all very grateful to be on this Earth and we all need to make the most of it.

LIAM

f Liam Hannah
@liamhannah767

> "Maybe the teen years are the years we can learn easily...we can make the most of opportunities while we're young."

RUBEN,

18, Huddersfield,

England

"I can show everyone what people with a disability are able to do with their future."

My dad found these scripts online about a Superman play and something about them made me interested and excited to have a go at acting. I am incredibly lucky because my parents run a theatre company for kids with disabilities, so they were in a great position to give me advice about getting some work.

My first job was to narrate a programme about three people with Down's syndrome. One who's a swimmer – in fact, that was me because I'm a really strong swimmer; one who's a surfer; and one who does drama. The programme was about the three of us.

Then I put myself forward for some work on *Newsround*, the children's news show on Children's BBC. I was reporting about children with disabilities in the cinema. One of my reports was about a girl with Down's syndrome who was enjoying the film too much and making too much noise which made it too loud for other people watching films. My news report was about how theatres and cinemas could be more welcoming for children with disabilities. I talked to the people at the *Lion King* who made sure they were as friendly as possible for the whole audience. They had a special pack to give out to children to explain what was happening when other children made a lot of noise, which I thought was great.

Then I heard about auditions for *The Dumping Ground*, a drama series about children living in a care home. We were on holiday in Devon when I heard from the casting director that I had a part. I thought she meant for one episode, but it was a five-month season! Now I tell my mum and dad I'm richer than them...

I enjoy everything about being in *The Dumping Ground*, from making new friends to the technical side. This has encouraged me to start making my own films on my iPad. I sometimes make a full video and a trailer and edit it on the editing suite on my iPad. I write songs as well. I learn by doing. I hope I'm breaking stereotypes at the same time.

Star of the Show:

YOU

I have also done another documentary which was hard-hitting. I went to Moldova and saw these institutions where people lived with all sorts of disabilities: cerebral palsy, Down's syndrome, autism…all types of conditions and different ages. I reported on them and about Lumos, a charity supported by J.K. Rowling that was trying to change the terrible conditions there.

It was very upsetting. The children there only had one toy each and were very poor. I also visited an amazing special school that the Lumos charity had funded. I met a boy in a wheelchair and asked him what he wanted to be when he was older. He said he wanted to be a policeman and I said to him, 'You can be the first policeman in Moldova in a wheelchair.'

I want to do more documentaries. I want to make challenging reports about people with disabilities. I work with a film crew who are all women with disabilities themselves. Some people are really kind to people with disabilities like me, and some people aren't. When they're not, it's unkind and unfair.

I went to a mainstream high school where I was bullied sometimes. They used a special education room for people with learning issues. This included me, and some of the others would stamp on my feet, trip me over and call me names. They did it in a way that wasn't obvious. They stopped me doing things and stopped me socializing. I was the first child with Down's syndrome in that school. It felt like I spent my whole time trying to fight against preconceptions.

I stuck it out there. I came out of school with GCSEs but no friends. I said to myself, 'I never have to do that again,' and I didn't look back.

I'm so pleased with how I've done since I've left school. When I'm not acting, I work at a sports centre as a sports coach assistant for swimming, badminton and table tennis.

My favourite part of life now is being with the friends I've made. I like my acting jobs, working with people with a disability. I want people to watch something I'm on and I want to inspire them. Then I can be an inspiring actor with a disability who can show everyone what people with a disability are able to do with their future.

Everyone in my old high school watched *The Dumping Ground* so now I'm famous there. I want to get even more famous and earn even more money!

This gives me a great feeling. People have preconceptions of what children with Down's can or can't do. I'm here to prove them wrong. In primary school, the teacher said to Mum, 'What do you think Ruben's going to do when he leaves school?' and she said, 'At the moment he's wants to be a rock star.' The teacher looked really shocked and Mum thought, 'Just you wait and see.'

RUBEN

"Children with Down's used to be hidden away. What I'm doing is the opposite."

IMANI,

18, Los Angeles, USA

"If students of color hear they are growing up to be nothing, that's what will happen and that's what I want to change."

Growing up, one of the biggest challenges I faced was that people would constantly ask me 'what I was'. I am Lebanese and Afro-Guatemalan, and even though this is a beautiful combination, I faced a struggle growing up, coming to terms with my unusual ethnic background.

I am a Latina who doesn't speak Spanish perfectly. I'm too white-passing to look like a 'typical' Afro-Latina. I am an 'Americanized' Arab, not relating to the 'traditional' Arab culture.

My fair skin and big curly hair were what often led people to question the complexity of my ethnic mix. As a little girl, I was embarrassed at some of the reactions I got from other kids who had trouble even pronouncing the countries my parents were from, let alone where they were located. I would simply tell people I was black and white because it was easier that way, even though that meant rejecting significant aspects of my cultures.

In elementary school, one of the things that started to dawn on me during the annual tribute lectures on September 11 was how many bad feelings there were about Islam. That made me shy away from that side of myself. Then, when I went to high school, which had a high population of Latin people, compared to my friends I felt like the white girl in my group.

I struggled to learn Spanish properly and struggled to speak it without stuttering because I felt I wasn't doing it justice. I keep working towards it and practice it, but still at the back of my mind I know that because I never fully learned it growing up it is harder for me to be fluent now.

Last year I was awarded a scholarship to study abroad in Egypt for a while and I came to know the significance of what it means to be an Arab woman. This gave me a sense of pride and hope, to see the women there persevere in the conditions they found themselves in despite the many limitations that face Muslim and Hijabi women. There were a lot of unspoken rules and regulations for women: the oldest daughter in a family could not go out without a curfew and her younger brother would be a chaperone. This seemed to be a male-dominated culture but my female friends who wore hijabs, despite the difficulties they faced, felt proud of their religion and culture. They showed me that I too could be proud of every aspect of my ethnicity and accept myself as an Arab-Afro-Latina-American woman who is ready to promote the same acceptance of all races in others.

I aim to promote acceptance of race and gender through artistic work. One of my latest projects was a documentary I made with the organization Global Girl Media. Through the experiences I've had working with the women in Global Girl, I have been able to gain a new sense of establishing my own identity through art and connections I've made with people.

I have made a film about the drag queen community in Los Angeles. There's a lot of controversy about darker queens who don't get as much work as lighter queens and can't get their make-up done properly, because of a lack of choice of shades in the make-up industry. The film explores colorism and social isolation for this community. The drag queens I interviewed confirmed that a lot of drag culture is white. They talked about using activism in their performance, coming to terms with their identity and being happy in their skin. One said that their family often referred to them as 'pocha', a term that refers to being 'whitewashed' in Spanish. Men are meant to be the strong ones, the heads of the family; concepts established by the ideology we know as machismo. While these cultural standards and ideologies excluded them, they were careful not to feel excluded from their culture, so he researched and read history and became educated in his own roots so that no one could take that away from him.

When I heard this, I decided that I didn't know enough about Guatemala and Lebanon and I started exploring my own heritage. I didn't want people to tell me, 'You're not really Latina, you're not really Arab.' Now I can say I know my history; I know what happened to my family to get us where we are today.

I have also started campaigning at school. I have promoted awareness among underclassmen of color, so they could have a head start when applying for college. Privilege has a lot to do with success when applying for college. Our school system has been set up in ways that mean students of color feel not good enough and not confident enough. I want to change the message, to go past the mental barrier that says people of color are not capable of advance placement classes. If someone hears they are growing up to be nothing, that's what will happen and that's what I want to change.

I am going to UC Berkeley in the fall to study global management and journalism. When I work, what I want to do with my career is to lend power to other people. Never underestimate the power of young people: we are young, we are naïve, but we have a voice; we have recourse to social media; we have the power of our own minds and the millennial perspective. The way we are is different from our own parents. We may be underestimated and underappreciated, but that's why we need to sound our voices.

So many people, even in our own age group, don't take the time to listen to each other, to explore our diversity of opinions and backgrounds. In America, people have so many different ideas and beliefs. We need to be heard. There is nothing useful about standing idly and being angry with each other. We think we are doing something, expressing ourselves, but we are just standing and moving in a circle.

I think that in my generation there are people who are aware of what's going on and people who would like to be aware but are not fully enlightened. We can see social media and Twitter updates and jump on what we see, but we can also look at the research and use that to form a cogent argument. We can base beliefs on facts, so we are not just biased. Educating ourselves on what we deem most important and developing our own authentic beliefs is what can truly empower us and help establish a platform on which we can see ourselves represented.

No matter what kinds of limitations our environment or circumstances may place upon us, there are no barriers around our minds. Our free thought can't be taken away by anyone. Our minds are sacred places and, as young people, we have time to learn. It can be one of our goals to be educated and open to the abundance of ideas that make up this world around us.

IMANI

@itsimanisalazar
@missmaani

"Never underestimate the power of young people. We have a voice, we have time to learn."

GURO,

13, Bergen, Norway

"I persuaded the makers of the pop video that girls are not just for show."

When I was 5, my favourite TV show was *Mickey Mouse Clubhouse.* I noticed that it was always Mickey who was driving the car and the girls were always sitting in the passenger seat, or even in the back seat. I asked my dad why this was, and he hadn't noticed this before. In our family my mum and dad both drive, so I thought it was odd.

Then, when I was 9, I saw all these mannequins in a shopping centre and I noticed something that my mum hadn't spotted. All the boy mannequins were doing handstands and the girl mannequins were just sitting still looking at them. I was thinking, 'That's not fair.'

I asked my mum to help me write to the newspaper about it. The manager of the mall asked me to come and make a display of one of the girls doing a handstand. I changed the clothes on one of the girls for one of the boys, so that the girl also could do a handstand. That was fun. I was very happy with that.

When I was a bit older, I went to buy a backpack. I wanted a light blue one and all the backpacks for girls were pink. I thought, 'All these backpacks in a store – why is there nothing for both genders?' If you choose a boy backpack, you will be teased. If you take the girlie one, you will just not be being yourself. I ended up buying a brown leather backpack, similar to the one my mum and dad used in the 1980s.

Then, when I was 11, I saw this video by a very popular Norwegian pop duo. All the girls love them. I was at home sick, watching TV, and I saw something I didn't think was right in the video. All the boys were doing back flips into the swimming pool, swimming and skating, and all the girls were just standing around trying to look good. The girls weren't doing anything that was fun, and I wanted the girls to have fun.

I made a video of me saying I don't think it was right that the girls were doing nothing and the boys doing everything. Then I sent the video to the newspaper and the pop group's management saw what I had done. They said they didn't agree and that they didn't want to change the music video.

When I heard this, I started a campaign. It was called #Ikketilpynt, meaning 'not for show'. I was saying that girls are not just for decoration. We don't just stand there and try to look nice. I wanted people to use the hashtag when they do something cool or something a little different.

I couldn't believe it! It spread everywhere on Twitter, Facebook and Instagram. It was used by politicians and broadcasters. I was on national TV and in the national newspapers and in the newspapers in Denmark.

Finally the music company decided to re-edit the video.

It was amazing. All the people stood together and made a change we didn't think was possible.

I don't want children or adults to think what we are able to do is different for different genders. Girls can do all these things that boys are shown doing. If we don't look at the small things and argue for change, we can't change the big things.

I think I grew up always knowing this. We are quite a modern family, but my parents say I have inspired them. Sometimes you just look around and know something is wrong.

After the hashtag campaign, TED Talks asked me if I would come and talk about gender equality. I did this speech in English to tell all the people what I care about. The local politicians then gave me a gender equality prize. Later, I gave another talk, and in the audience were almost all the mayors in Norway. I think people now understand me better when I say what's actually right and what's wrong.

Still now I'm always looking out for things, very small things, that need changing. In books, it's often boys doing the cool stuff, and the girls who cry when a snake comes into class. I told my teacher about this book I was reading, and he said, 'It's just how it is,' but I don't think it has to be.

The topics I look at may seem pretty small. It's all about being yourself and then you can do whatever you like. You should be the person you are, not the stereotype. If there's something that you want to do that's not typical, you should do it. If you want to do something different, just be who you want to be.

GURO

#Ikketilpynt (Norwegian)
#notforshow (English)

"If we don't look at the small things and argue for change, we can't change the big things."

GAVIN,

18, Ohio, USA

"I felt like an underdog but, once I found a way to express myself, I didn't need to rebel anymore."

When I was 10, I started playing the piano. This means I don't have that rigorous knowledge of technique that you have if you start at 5, when most professional pianists would have started.

The area that I'm from is a very rural, poor town in south-east Ohio, so the only teachers available to me were those who taught kids the elementary basics. This meant I was largely self-taught. Then I lucked out and a teacher came to my local area who had just graduated from the Royal Conservatory in London, so I started classical lessons about three years ago. This was when I learned my first classical piece and was the first time I received any technical training.

I think 10 was the right time for me to start; I think if my parents had pushed me into it earlier, it might have put me off. Because I started late, my playing has grown organically. It has become more and more part of my life and more and more important to me. I never thought in a thousand years I would be able to say this, but I will soon be going to the Cincinnati Conservatory of Music, my top goal, to study piano performance. In fact, after I'd passed the auditions, my new piano professor at the conservatory actually wanted to be my professor because she grew up in a similar area and knew that there weren't opportunities for aspiring pianists in Appalachia.

I have achieved my goal even though I haven't had a long performance history, unlike so many others. I've done recitals every few months. I've learned Brahms, Bach and Haydn, and some jazz just for fun, but I haven't trodden the path so many others have taken.

It wasn't always my dream to be a musician. I wanted to be an architect for a while, then fell into music more and more. Playing the piano sort of came easily to me at the beginning, but I certainly wasn't a prodigy. I just sort of enjoyed it and could understand what my teacher was telling me and that encouraged me to keep going.

The piano has definitely helped get me through my teenage years. It's an emotional de-stressor. It's so expressive emotionally and creatively that it helps me find what I want to do and allows me to go home and improvise. It is something I can do daily that gives me purpose – for a lot of kids my age, school is their entire path.

When I was a kid growing up, I would always make friends with the awkward kids. I had a few friends who were ruffian types. I have had friends I've had to distance myself from after they started to get into trouble at school or get too far into drugs or partying. I had to keep focused. Playing the piano was central in allowing me to do that.

I found that I enjoyed the process of studying academically to express yourself – having something you like that really interests you and you are able to dissect. I realized in 6th grade* that I wanted to be a professional musician and I was in the talented and gifted building at school when that happened. The talented and gifted program was hugely valuable for me and let me know that I could do whatever I set my mind to. It was my escape from the monotonous life of normal school and really

---

*   Ages 11–12.

promoted creativity. It was huge in my development. We were going to this careers program at school and at that moment I thought, 'I really enjoy music.' The teacher had written up on the board, 'I want to be a…' and then a blank. That's when I realized I wanted to be a professional musician and since then I haven't had any second doubts.

I don't come from a family of professional musicians, though we have always been into music. My family always played all sorts of music on the radio and I had a very broad musical experience growing up. My aunt played piano as a hobby and my grandma as well. My dad plays drums for fun. I found out after I decided to be a pianist that my great-grandmother actually attended the Conservatory of Bethlehem in Pennsylvania and was a pianist herself.

I believe if you enjoy doing something, you humble yourself in the process. When you think of the masters, you can't begin to perceive the hours it's taken for them to get to that level. Understanding that tradition of excellence, you have to humble yourself to this altar of music. When you feel you are good, then look at the people even higher than you. That's all about breaking down your expectations and your ego. It makes you a better person.

When you're a kid, you have no self-consciousness. You don't really understand that you're not great. When you're a teenager, you're self-conscious with yourself anyway. You need to get past that. You have to understand where you're at and where you want to be. Once you avoid getting discouraged because you think you're not very good, the process is beneficial, and you really enjoy it.

Since I was 10, music has been such a big part of my life and this has had a big impact on my teenage years. The systematic plodding through middle school or high school was not for me. I rebelled against that and, if I hadn't had this goal to achieve, I might have rebelled even more. Music allowed me to go to college instead of high school and to feel more of an individual, and once I found a way to express that I didn't need to rebel any more.

When I went to the audition at the Conservatory and listened to people rehearsing, I thought, 'Oh my gosh, I don't belong here.' I didn't think I did well in my auditions. I was missing notes. I didn't think I was at that level. I thought I had done so badly that I came home and made plans to go to another school. When I heard I'd got in, I shouted it from the stars, running into my mum's bedroom when she was asleep to tell her. I think a lot of my concern was self-doubt. I had started late and I felt I had a lack of ability. I thought if they gave me a place, I would get chewed up in there.

A lot of my friends are still undecided about what they want to do. I think that's OK. Everyone will find something they are passionate about. Get out there and try something. I felt that way too for a long time. Picture yourself doing something you enjoy and what it is that could lead you there.

For the past two or three years I have stopped feeling mediocre. I have stopped comparing myself with the kids who were prodigies. I have pushed past that. I don't think I'm exceptional. I had been improvising and making sounds when I was 2, 3 and 4, and I wish someone had noticed. Maybe I could have been one of those kids playing in Carnegie Hall, one of the prodigy children, but my parents were divorcing, getting remarried and divorcing again. Too much going on.

I see my path as the underdog, alternative path, not being raised into music and studying it at a top level. This path has its own perseverance and patience about it. It's been less about technique, more about passion. I believe that it's very rare that prodigies are born. They are often created by regimented teachers and parents. I am glad I took the alternative route. I have had the opportunity to have friends and lightsaber battles and play video games and hang out in the park and become a more rounded person in general.

A family friend, a guy that I really look up to, said to me once, 'To feel like you belong, you must first believe that you belong.' This has helped me a lot to feel like I belong in a place where there are so many reasons to feel like I don't belong. It's advice I would give anyone.

I would also say, if you feel like an underdog, accept your alternative route. I think a lot of self-discovery comes from feeling like an underdog. Lean into it and do things your own way but take note of what others are doing effectively. While you may want to prove yourself to the world, I think that the only person that you need to prove anything to is yourself. That will always get you further.

GAVIN

@gavindavis_00

> "If you feel like an underdog, accept your alternative route. Lean into it and do things your own way."

MATILDA,

13, Washington, DC, USA

"You can't judge someone by their clothes. People should do what they want with their bodies."

I always believe there's more to a person than what they wear. You can't judge someone by their clothes. People should do whatever they want with their bodies. I tell my friends they're beautiful. No one is ugly; we are all unique. No student should compare themselves to other students. If people put time and effort into mean comments when someone posts a picture and says, 'She looks disgusting,' I think their action is disgusting.

I see these make-up videos for 5-year-olds, with four palettes costing $50, and I think, 'They did not pay for these themselves.' This is not right. My friend said this 5-year-old was using make-up better than she was, and I said, 'That's not the point. She shouldn't be using make-up.' If I don't like the way it feels on my face, maybe they don't either. Putting something on your face to hide your face is like putting on a mask, in order not to show your true emotions.

I think all these videos of women getting into shape, women who started off as 'ugly'…I think these women are beautiful before the make-up and the 'transformation'. I want to reinforce positive thoughts in other people. If you tell someone they look amazing, it can make their day.

When you're an adult, your attitude is locked and loaded. You don't change much then. I think being a teenager is about grounding your attitude in elementary school, then shaping your attitude in middle school. The middle school era is when you can learn how to have strong arguments and that prepares you for high school.

It's uncomfortable being a teenager. You're finding yourself, you're seeing what you are into, trying to figure out who you are. It's important to be mature but not mature at the same time. It's a time to focus on having fun and also to get the grades you need for later life. Being a teenager opens a world of learning.

I spend time thinking about what I feel strongly about. I always tell people to have their own opinions, and not to have other people's opinions influence their own. I like to think that I do my best to affect the world in a positive way. I try my hardest to do what's right.

Not using social media is a decision I have made. I prefer to keep my life private. I think social media could be a great platform to post on, but it doesn't do much because everyone all over is doing it. This means there's too much. Also, if people are just watching videos, they are doing nothing.

When people see a 13-year-old teenager, they don't necessarily think, 'This person is going to be mature,' but I have lots of strong opinions. I try to keep my environment clean. I've had countless arguments with people in the past, like about the importance of trees and not taking care of them enough. There used to be 63 trillion trees on the planet and there are now only 3 trillion. It's important to keep our environment safe and clean. A clean environment with no trash makes you feel good. If it smells nice, it is nice.

I would love to work as a vet or a zoologist, rescuing and rehabilitating animals. The stuff that they go through dealing with humans is stupid.

Being a teenager is about looking around, then getting yourself together. It's a mistake not to look beyond yourself. I have strong opinions about science, books and movies. I love to look at astronomy and quantum mechanics and figure out what's going on.

It's very hard to understand science, but when you do, it makes the difference and we need to make a difference. Science is everything. People constantly say, 'When are we going to use science?' and the answer is 'All the time'.

MATILDA

"I tell my friends they're beautiful. No one is ugly; we are all unique."

NIAMH,

15, Liverpool, England

"A lot of teenagers in society are struggling to be themselves ... I want to give them a sense that the future will be all right."

I have always known I was bisexual. I remember going to parties and being around people who were strictly into boys and I just felt different. I felt comfortable and I felt like I was me, but I felt different from them.

It's hard to explain. One minute I go from being the biggest tomboy you have met to being a girly girl. I'm in the middle. I find that magazines and TV will be talking about Zac Ephron and I am going, 'Look at Vanessa Hudgens.' They never talked about the girl side of things and I did.

My parents always said no matter what I did, they would be supportive. When I came out to them last year, they said they were proud of me and that they felt that people wouldn't treat me any differently. It was at a New Year's Eve party and the whole family were round. I tried to bring it into the conversation casually and they were like, 'Oh, OK…' and then, 'We didn't know, but that's fine.' Pretty much the response at school has been the same. Society has moved on, though there are still some very opinionated people about. I've heard some negative things, but not necessarily directed towards me. I'm quite lucky.

If I was to show any weakness, I know for a fact that this would be picked up on straight away. I think how easy it is to come out is dependent on your confidence levels, family life and where you are in the world. If you feel comfortable within yourself, then have no fear. If you feel safe, then just do it.

I am in the Sea Cadets and I have been put on the front cover of their magazine and talked to them coming out. I have seen this as an opportunity to make it known that any negative responses wouldn't be OK. I am really supported there. The Cadets are a big part of my life. To be honest, if I hadn't done what I have done, I wouldn't have been me. I wouldn't have been authentic. I know that there are a lot of teenagers in modern society who are still struggling to be themselves. Things are moving fast, but they still do struggle. I want to give them a sense that the future will be all right.

I believe that if anyone has problem with what I have done, then that is their problem not mine. I know I have my family, and any friends who had a problem with it weren't really my friends.

Because I am so 'out', I have had people come up to me asking what I think they should do. Some are older, some are younger, some are the same age. I have made quite a few friends just by being there for people. I tell them that if they face hostility, it's just from those few people who need to educate themselves into becoming more accepting of what they don't see as normal, because it is normal.

To be honest, I think quite a big part of any negativity stems from religion. There's an ignorance and a feeling of people not wanting to know about what they don't already know.

Thanks to social media, people now know that a lot of big, big people are very accepting of LGBT+. I have been obsessed with a band called Fifth Harmony. One of the girls in the band, Lauren, came out as bisexual roughly when I did. She has always been someone I looked up to and is now an authority figure on the matter. She's helped show that people can do and be what they want. In the past it was 'be who you want to be but be quiet about it.'

I don't think I'm anything special but, to my mind, if you're not being authentically you, what's the point? You're here for the amount of time you're here. You might as well be here in a way that makes you happy.

NIAMH

@tumblrdodie
@niamh.adamson

"Because I am so 'out', I have had people come up to me asking what I think they should do."

HANNAH,

17, Arlington, Virginia, USA

"We bring people with disabilities into the general community and learn to see life through a different lens."

At school I'm part of Best Buddies, an organization that pairs together individuals with and without disabilities in a year-long friendship. I joined the club my sophomore year of high school, became the Wakefield High School chapter's Vice President last year, and this year I am the President of our chapter. I think Best Buddies has turned me into a better person and I have learned a lot about myself. The most important thing I've learned is that everyone is really similar; even if some people look or act different, everyone's the same on the inside. I do hope being involved has turned me into a less selfish person, though I hope I wasn't too selfish to begin with!

It's great for all of us to have this experience: Best Buddies gives the students who are buddied up an automatic best friend. Buddy pairs go out and do stuff together a few times a month. Last year, my buddy, James, and I would hang out at his house, go bike riding, and then walk to a local diner and get lunch and milkshakes. Afterwards, he would read to me. At the end of the year, I asked James to the Best Buddies Prom, so he had that real experience within the school community that most people with disabilities miss out on. We had an awesome time!

Some of our buddies are in sports teams at school: basketball, soccer and cheerleading. It's cool to see them being involved. We are trying to bring whole-school awareness about people with disabilities. Our school has a whole program called MIPA (Multi-Intervention Program for Students with Autism). For International Autism Awareness Week, different days, people would carry around or wear items to exemplify different parts of autism.

One day, everyone wore sunglasses to help our school community understand what it feels like to have sensory issues.

If you learn about how someone else lives, you get to see life through a different lens. I get the chance to hang out with people one on one and truly learn lessons about the values every person brings to the table. Questions always help anyone learn more about anything. I have learned to ask a lot of questions and I like listening to other people's stories.

Treating people with disabilities as your equal is extremely important. People in Wakefield's Best Buddies chapter are in high school and should be treated as such. When people talk down to our buddies or treat them like babies, it dehumanizes them and suggests that they are not on the same level as the general education kids. That is blatantly not true. I have a connective tissue disorder with my joints, called Hypermobile Ehlers-Danlos syndrome, and I have to go to physical therapy once or twice a week. My condition is invisible; you cannot tell I have it just by looking at me. Last year I was having a hard time with my knees and couldn't walk that well, but I knew that many people have more difficulties than me and that helped me appreciate all I could do.

The role of Best Buddies is to bring people with disabilities into the general community, as they have historically been very segregated. Some have faced bullying: there are many people at our school who make fun of them. I think people are scared of what they don't know. Best Buddies is trying to end the stigma. I think that the teenage years are a good time to learn these lessons in life and gain understanding, because this will make you open-minded and learn more about yourself and the world around you. You can create good habits for the rest of your life. I think if more young people were a part of this incredible organization, we would have a more open society. Best Buddies has made me more open. It's taught me that just because you don't know what's going on with other people's lives doesn't mean you can judge someone.

HANNAH

 @omgits_hannahg

"The most important thing I've learned is that everyone is really similar; even if some people look or act different, everyone's the same on the inside."

MOLLIE,

20, Dover, England

"I want to change the mindset that the way some people look is not OK. Use what's different about you in your favour."

In this society people are very quick to judge. There's a negative portrayal of body types and images and it's not right.

When I was 17, I launched a campaign to showcase that it's OK to be who you are.

I have always struggled with my body image. It can be awful when people are prejudiced against you. I thought I would stand up for myself, give myself a voice and hopefully other people will be inspired by it.

My inspiration is the view that we are all equal. There is nothing to be prejudiced about. It is impossible to be genetically identical, unless you're a twin, so expecting us to be aesthetically the same doesn't make any sense.

I was bullied at primary school and halfway through secondary school, for being overweight. This affected me a great deal as a young girl. I didn't understand where this criticism was coming from and I took this as an attack on my personality as well as an attack on me personally.

I finally lost the weight as a teenager and it proved to the people who were bullying me that there was nothing wrong with me. They could see I was a great person; it was just that I was slightly overweight. When you're 11 years old, it's not normal to feel personally attacked and to feel horrible about yourself. It's not something you want to be feeling.

I want to change the mindset that the way some people look is not OK. People can be racist; there are a lot of immigrants in Dover who can face abuse. There can be bad feelings against homeless people. I'm thinking we are all equal. You shouldn't be attacking these people. I help out with soup kitchens and I know that a lot of people assume the homeless are drunk or on drugs, but in reality they have a lot of different problems. These can be family problems or financial problems. We are too quick to judge.

I think when social media first started everyone was very excited about it. People felt positive for a while, but then even celebrities were getting bullied and negative comments. Half the time people don't know what they are saying. It's something they have inside their heads and they post it without thinking. They haven't got the person in front of them. I also think it's due to the press, magazines, models, adverts on the telly, film stars, with all the photoshopping, editing and make-up – even for guys, who now need to be muscly, with six packs. The message we need to share is that you can be who you are and still be beautiful.

I come from a huge family spanning different cultures from Australia to Wales. We have a lot of different attitudes, but the whole family is very accepting of how people look.

I use this to motivate me. When I lost those that weight, I still didn't like the way people were talking about others and I'd say, 'Stop doing that!' Within my social group, we agreed not to pick on anyone. I launched a campaign on body image when we were in the sixth form.* We invited people to come down and see what we were doing, people were attracted to it and it caught on.

I organized my friends into a flash mob. We spread out this huge sheet and put different shapes on it to resemble the different shapes and sizes that people are. We were trying to spread the message, subconsciously, that we are all the same. We all wore

---

*   Ages 16–18.

tee-shirts about body image. We got people to come and take part, decorating the sheet with different shapes and then sharing it on social media. We made a film about what we'd done with Fixers, the organization that helps young people campaign about the issues that matter to them. It was one small event, but I hope we made people think. Ever since, I've been spreading the same message.

More than being accepting of everyone, I think teenagers should use what's seen as negative as their biggest motivation to achieve. Use what's different about you in your favour. Everyone has a quirk – we have to embrace them, these things that are part of who we are that will help you fulfil yourself and become who you want to be.

MOLLIE

@molliegregory_

> "I think teenagers should use what's seen as negative as their biggest motivation to achieve."

5...

DISCOVERING MY PASSION

BETTY,

13, Utrecht,

The Netherlands

"I applied to be CEO of Greenpeace International when I was 11. I wanted them to know that people my age had opinions too."

When Kumi Naidoo, who was CEO of Greenpeace International, left his job, he made a really inspiring speech about the problems in the world and how we need to work together to solve them. I was listening to what he was saying at a conference where I went with my dad and felt completely inspired. I was only 11 and I decided to apply for Kumi's job. I knew I wouldn't be chosen because Greenpeace is against child labour! But I wanted them to know that people my age had opinions too and we could also work to make change. In fact, I believe young people have an advantage – we don't overthink things in the way that adults do.

I received a great reply from Kumi and from Greenpeace telling me they really liked my letter, along with a book – a really nice story about how people can change the world. They said, 'When you are older, there will be a job here for you.'

I think we can change the world. I have been to conferences and I've heard a lot about helping people and looking after the environment. Learning about the environment really touches me. I hate how it's going: how people treat animals as if they are different from us and not as important as us. They are used by us when they are living things in the same way that we are. I'm also concerned about how we treat people of different races and anybody who's different to us in any way.

I think it's important to spend some of your time fighting for what is right, not just doing things for your own pleasure.

I am on the youth council of War Child in the Netherlands, an organization that helps children who are suffering because of conflict in different countries. We meet every month in Amsterdam. Me and two other girls there called Rosa and Lynn decided we should try to get the War Child office to be environmentally friendly. They were using coffee that wasn't Fairtrade; they used a lot of plastic. We were arguing that they should make changes. War Child do really listen.

I'm vegan. A lot of the other kids don't know this, and when they find out, they are often not interested or think it's not important. They don't see why they should be vegan because it's not always convenient; they know it would make things a lot harder for themselves. It's not nice if my friends say I am becoming boring talking about it, but I do think I have to tell them about what I believe in. I try not to talk about it every day.

I had been vegetarian for a couple of years as I hate it when animals are exploited. I know that factory farming is a number-one contributor to climate change. At home we almost only eat vegan or vegetarian food.

At primary school, I took part in the night-time walk called 'The Night of the Refugees'. It was the length of a marathon. We walked through the night and raised a few thousand euros to help refugees. What I liked was that I knew we were doing it for the good of other people who needed our help. We had a page on the internet and people could pledge money. My mum thought I would drop out because I was the youngest person on the walk. She came along to take me home when I'd had enough, but we actually finished it. Because I was the youngest, the TV people interviewed me at 3 am. It was really hard, and I told them that. We started at midnight and went on till 11 in the morning. Then I had to go to school the next day…

When I'm older, I would like to be an environmentalist or a human rights lawyer. You're fighting for something and doing something useful and learning, all at the same time.

I believe teenagers everywhere are not helpless, even if they sometimes feel they can't make any changes. If your heart is in it and you try your best, you will get to places and do things in your life.

I think we can change the world and make it a better place for everybody, all creatures and people. I think we can do this peacefully. Some people think they can't change things because they are just one person, but if everyone thought that, nothing would get done. If everyone did one small thing, there would be a massive change. It's as simple as that.

BETTY

> "I believe young people have an advantage — we don't overthink things in the way that adults do."

JESSE,

15, New York, USA

"I get comments about my height at least six times a day but I love being tall. I even bleach my hair blonde to stand out more."

In many ways I am a typical teenager; I love music and I play video games. What makes me different is that I am one of around 3000 people in the world who are seven feet tall.

I have always been very, very positive about my height. I love being tall. It means I get a lot of attention, which I love, and it's always a conversation starter. Being this tall feels unique and, outside of professional basketball players, I have never met anyone taller than me. I have never been teased about it, but then I can loom over most people. I think it's important to express who you are and show your individuality: I even bleach my hair blonde just to stand out more.

Because of the amount of people who come up to me and talk to me, I have no choice but to be social; however, I enjoy it entirely. My parents are very social, so I've grown up finding it easy to talk with people.

I get comments about my height at least six times a day. Everywhere I go people say, 'You probably hear this all the time…' I enjoy the comments except when they start commenting on what I should do or how I should be. Because I'm only 15 and 7 feet, I'm not bulky, I'm pretty skinny, and some people comment on that, but with five or six days a week training that is starting to change. People give different reactions in different countries. I went travelling with my dad and in France I could see everyone whispering into their hands and pointing. In Spain no one batted an eye. England was the worst: this woman just came up to me and told me, 'You should take anti-growth hormones; you're not normal.' I just laughed. I thought it was kind of funny that she was so angry about it! Since then my dad and I have started a 'Not Normal' website. I'm thinking of putting it on a tee-shirt: 'Not Normal'.

We should embrace our differences.

Until my height really became part of me, I had never considered myself to be that much of a sports player. Then I thought it could be an amazing thing. I started playing basketball a few years ago and love it.

I was scouted at a NY Knicks basketball camp by the Riverside Hawks in Manhattan, one of the oldest AAU* teams in the country. When I went to my first practice, I was incredibly anxious. The truth was I knew very little about basketball. It was nerve-wracking. I went in soccer gear because I didn't have basketball clothing. It was difficult because everyone knew how to dribble around, lay-up, do all these crazy movements – and I could barely bounce a ball.

Another thing that was hard was that, because I was tall, everyone expected me to automatically play really, really well. After a while, I started to learn the ropes and it got easier and more fun and people started to trust me. It's a team sport and it's all about trust. I think what has really worked for me was – and is – commitment. Through commitment I have stuck with it for about

---

*   Amateur Athletic Union.

three years and over that time it has not necessarily got easier, but I have improved and have more confidence. The game has slowed down for me: when you are in an actual game, it can be so fast that you really don't know what is going on, but now I can see it. It has also become more fun.

I have got better and better and stronger and fitter. I learned a lot of skills, especially because in my first proper season I was thrown into a 75-game season with one of the most successful teams in the city. I had never played in a team before and it was scary, but they supported me and wanted me to improve, and gradually I have felt more and more a part of the team. The main thing with Riverside was that most of my teammates have been playing for almost ten years, and some of them had been playing together for four or five years, but I feel everyone has a role and I found my role within the team. I'm the big man, of course, which is all about getting the rebounds, blocking people, hopefully scoring some points and general intimidation. I have had to learn to be aggressive, which is something that really doesn't come naturally to me.

Looking back, I don't think right off the block it's possible to be amazing. It really is about dedication and hard work at the end of the day.

I'm transferring to a new school this fall that is very sports orientated, and I am going there to specifically play basketball, but also hopefully to get me into a better position to get into a Division 1 college. I won't know anyone there. Sometimes I get a little nervous about what they will think of me, and then I realize it doesn't really matter – it's not as if I could hide if I wanted to.

If you are comfortable with your own body and who you are, it doesn't matter what everyone else thinks. If you have done all you can to express who you are and what you think and if people don't like that, you probably shouldn't be hanging out with those people.

I feel genuinely lucky to live in New York City where everyone is very different in his or her own way. It's not a city for conforming. One hundred percent, living here has strengthened me as a person and so has playing basketball. To begin with in basketball I didn't know anything or anybody, but the more comfortable you get, the easier it is, and the more confident you get, the better you get. I'm not so scared of new things as a result of these experiences.

Dad's six foot three and Mum's six foot so I was always going to be tall. I am a natural non-conformist, and I don't ever want to feel like I have to fit in. I had a friend who was all about that – always wanting to fit in with new trends at the right time. If you live like that, it's not really your own life. It's not so bad if you actually like the new trends, of course, but if you're not happy with the person who you are, then I don't think you should force yourself to try to be this perfect person and conform to those expectations.

In my experience it's great for teenagers to try new things. If you enjoy them, even if you're not very good at them, the more you do them, the more confident you will feel about that certain thing, the more comfortable you will feel. And don't be afraid to fail. When I first started playing basketball, I did have a fear of failing, of course, and if I played horribly, I would bring myself down thinking about it. But at the end of the day, I've realized it's just a sport. I will keep playing, keep getting better. I definitely want to play college basketball; I'm not necessarily sure I want to be a professional basketball player, but we will see. What's most important is that I want to be in a good place. To be fit and happy is ambition in itself.

JESSE

> "If you are comfortable with your own body and who you are, it doesn't matter what everyone else thinks."

@jesseskyhigh
High school team:
@polybluedevils
AAU team:
@riversidehawksnyc
www.notnormal.life

Photograph of Jesse by Martin Crook

BILLY,

18, Los Angeles, USA

"I wore full make-up to high school every day. People would come up to me and compliment me on my eyebrows."

During high school, I had really bad acne and it kept getting worse. This started when I was 16 and continued for two years. I put on foundation to cover it up and that worked really well.

As I did this, I realized I actually loved make-up and what it can do. I went to high school with full make-up on every day. It took me an hour and a half to get my face done each morning. I started practicing on people at school and realized I was really good at it. I decided I wanted to pursue that as a career.

A boy doing make-up is different from a girl doing make-up. I was fortunate that at my school no one cared, and everyone was very accepting.

Until I had acne I had no idea what I wanted to do after school. I was thinking of going to college, as every teenager does, but as soon as I started doing make-up I was surprised how fast I picked it up. I practiced mostly on myself, but other people asked me to do it for them for homecoming, which I loved.

I had a smooth ride at school; honestly, a lot of the schools in DC are very open and PC. People would just go, 'Oh, wow, Billy's wearing make-up!' It was talked about – it was even in the school newspaper. People would come up to me and compliment me on my eyebrows. I liked that people were talking about me, and in a good way. I wanted to do something different and to be talked about. I have always wanted people to appreciate what I'm doing. I've always felt confident, and this transitioned into wearing make-up.

I didn't fully come out as gay until 10th or 11th grade.* I didn't need to because everyone knew and I was never bullied. As I said, I had a smooth ride. I loved cheerleading; I hated sport so this was a workout for me. I discovered that the reason I loved cheerleading was because I love performing and didn't like the acting path, but I loved being the centre of attention.

Without the acne, my love of make-up would have become obvious much more slowly. It was definitely a push for me to realize I can do what I wanted. In the back of my mind I do care what people think about my appearance, but I know it's my life.

As I was growing up, there was a lot of family drama. Divorce and other things during my childhood have made me an independent person and very strong. At 18 I am already living and working by myself.

My parents are very accepting of everything I do. I'm very fortunate for that. Without that, I couldn't do what I am doing with my career in make-up. I would probably be doing interior design and I honestly do love that but it's less personal for me.

I left high school early because Dad moved to LA. I knew this was the place I had to go to, to make my career happen. I moved

---

*   Ages 15–17.

here by myself and love being in an apartment in Hollywood by myself. I finished my schooling online. I feel very lucky because a lot of teens are very confused about what they want to do, and I have a strong passion for what I want. I'm 18 and I'm making money doing what I love. Such an amazing thing.

I've decided that I'm not going to college because I don't need to. I already have a client base of influencers on YouTube and Instagram with 500,000 to 5 million followers. I have 120,000 followers across all platforms. My style's pretty natural but very glam. The market is saturated, so I have to stand out to be seen and noticed. I've recently decided to start my own cosmetic brand. I want it to be made in America, not China, though it's definitely more expensive to do here. I'm very business savvy.

I have only once faced any abuse and that was in LA. People online sometimes say to me, 'Are you a girl or a boy?' A lot of people will be confused. A lot of people might be very sensitive about this, but to me it's nothing. I know who I am.

I think when you are a teenager is the most important time for change. I don't think people realize they need to love themselves for who they are when they are this age. You have to be fully accepting of yourself and this whole process is very important for a teenager. It's a time to try new things. If you don't like them, don't do them. If you don't like someone else doing them, it shouldn't matter to you because it's not your life.

I know I am going into a competitive industry, but my idea is to keep doing it, keep working on what is my number-one interest. Just because other people are doing it, why shouldn't I be doing it?

Kids and teenagers are so influenced by everything they see online. Social media is saturated with people trying to look perfect all the time. I try to project an image on social media which is not exactly perfect. This idea that everything is perfect is very damaging for teenagers: damaging and discouraging, especially for young girls.

What I do has helped me to realize the fakeness of social media. Some people are very open about their experiences, which helps others as well. I have motivational talks on my Instagram story and a lot of others talk about their past as well, to help other teenagers and stop them making the same mistakes.

BILLY

🐦 @Bly_Blu
📷 @boujeebilly

"I liked that people were talking about me, and in a good way. I wanted to do something different and to be talked about."

NATALIA,

17, Arlington,

Virginia, USA

"We are taking action together: for the environment, for our communities, for our safety. We are learning and making mistakes and making history all at the same time."

As teenagers, right now is when we can really figure out what we care about and where our passions lie. We are not set in our ways. We can see that our own personal actions can make a difference. I believe teenagers share this as a common thread.

My passion is for environmental conservation, which has been driven by the backpacking, kayaking and camping trips I have spent my life going on. I have a deep appreciation and love for nature. Between my freshman and sophomore years, I spent three weeks working on a conservation crew in three national forests in Oregon. With seven other teenagers, I helped make hiking trails accessible by uprooting invasive plants, moving fallen trees and building runoffs so that the trails wouldn't erode over time.

Those three weeks of work were three of the best in my life. Conservation work is a way for me to give back to the places that have given me so much, while also continuing to be immersed in the beauty of it all. As a junior, I spent six months interning at the Student Conservation Association, the same organization that led the conservation crew I was on. This gave me the opportunity to see what it's like to work in an environmental field, alongside professionals who are just as passionate about conservation as I am. We don't necessarily see its effects day to day, but climate change is a huge issue that everyone should be fighting. My time in nature has showed me this and it's now up to my generation and the ones after me to continue to fight for our planet. No matter what I do in college, or what profession I have later on in life, environmental conservation will always be my passion and priority.

It's not just me. My friends and the people I spend my time with are conscious of the world we are living in. Many of them are involved in youth groups and do community service and social action projects through them. Everyone is doing good in the world in their own way.

I am fortunate to live a well-off and content life, and knowing that I am helping other people to have the same opportunities and experiences is what motivates me. This drive to give others those opportunities is also why I want to be a social worker. My friends come to me for help and I love being there to support and guide them. I am happiest when I'm helping others, especially other teenagers, which is why I want to work with teens when I am older. Teenagers are the future of every generation and there is so much stress and hardship that we go through that isn't seen from the outside and that people tend to forget once they become adults. Even when I'm no longer a teenager, I know that young people will be those I will connect with most.

It's a tough time to be a teenager now, but there are so many opportunities for us to grab and take hold of – opportunities that wouldn't have been available ten years ago. We have so many ways to find our passion and be involved in the world. We have to take these opportunities and make them our own. We are a lot more connected through social media, so we are able to see things a lot quicker and are impacted more. This is why, for instance, I took part in the protests after the gunman opened fire at the Marjory Stoneman Douglas High School in Parkland, Florida, killing and injuring so many there.

I remember that I didn't properly take in what had happened when I first heard about the shooting. I wanted to feel a gut-wrenching pain and I didn't. We've had so much exposure from the news about shootings across the country that I didn't feel anything.

When I began reading stories of the individual victims, I realized that those students were just like the students I walk by every day in the hallways at my own high school. They could have easily been me and my friends. That community could have been mine.

I am part of a non-profit, international Jewish youth organization called BBYO that encourages Jewish teenagers to stay involved in their religion after their b'nai mitzvahs. Because of BBYO, I spend my weekends connecting with other Jewish teens and doing community service projects in my area. I am also an elected officer in my BBYO community, which has given me the opportunity to grow as a leader, to guide others, and learn how to work alongside my peers. Being a member and a leader in BBYO has guided me through high school; it has introduced me to a group of people who support me and has shown me that I love making a difference in other people's lives.

The shooting occurred the day before BBYO held its International Convention in Orlando, Florida. The convention brings in more than 3000 teenagers from across the country and the world. There were Parkland students there, and we had a few moments of silence for the victims. During the silence I could see teens in every part of the large ballroom room holding each other and grasping hands.

The shooting had occurred at a high school 1000 miles from my home, yet Parkland students were part of one of the most tight-knit communities that I am a part of. That really hit home for me.

Last spring, I took part in the March for Our Lives protests in Washington. Most of the protest was dedicated to listening to teenagers speak, tell their stories, read poems and sing. Watching teenagers my age command not just a room but the entire National Mall in Washington, DC, was incredible. It instilled so much drive and passion in teenagers around the country. It is what made the march stand apart from any others. Strangers were talking to each other, crying beside each other and complimenting each other's creative protest signs.

I am so grateful I got to be part of something so unforgettable, and that highlighted just how much teenagers are capable of. I witnessed that the strongest way to mobilize teenagers is with other teenagers. Knowing that participating in the March for

Our Lives was benefiting not only to peers and fellow teenagers just a cause they cared about, but a like them, is what I think cause that had personal meaning mobilized students the most.

School shootings aren't an abstract thought: they are something that could occur any day at any school in our country. We all know this. High school students across the United States share a common thread: we all spend seven hours a day, five days a week in school – schools that are equally vulnerable to tragedy.

I think that the response following Parkland – clearly so much bigger and stronger than any other response we have seen by those against gun violence – made complete sense. Victims of shootings in public spaces have no common thread connecting them. They all have different identities, different lives, and grieve in separate spaces with their own family and friends.

The victims of elementary school shootings are still young, and don't have the platform or capacity to make large-scale change. A high school, on the other hand, is a tight-knit, strong community, full of bright minds and future leaders. They care about the people who surround and support them in classes and on teams and have a network of support that spans the entire country.

I think it's easy for adults to assume that teenagers can't see the bigger picture, because they think we are wrapped up in the minute details of our generation. In some cases, this attitude might be valid, but most teenagers are making an impact in ways that aren't seen by adults. We are taking action together: for the environment, for our communities, for our safety. We are learning and making mistakes and making history all at the same time, preparing for when we lead the world ourselves.

NATALIA

"It's easy for adults to assume that teenagers can't see the bigger picture. Teenagers are making an impact in ways that aren't seen by adults."

TOLMEIA

(TOLLY DOLLY POSH),

18, Gloucestershire,

England

"I decided that ethics were more important than anything else in fashion and that I had to do something about this."

About six years ago I started my fashion blog. It was something to do for fun. I was interested in websites and wanted to get a feel for using them myself while focusing on a topic that I was hugely passionate about.

I was originally focused on fast fashion and celebrity style. It was all about colour and glamour and excitement. It was what I knew and was aware of because I hadn't ever been educated on sustainability.

Then, by chance, I watched a documentary called *The True Cost*. It was about who pays the true price for the cheap clothing that we buy: the cost to the environment, and the farmers and the factory workers who are exploited. The documentary was created after a garment factory in Bangladesh collapsed, killing more than 1000 workers. Watching it really opened my mind. I decided that ethics were more important than anything else in fashion and that I had to do something about this.

I think being a teenager played a big part in my decision. I knew that previous generations had messed things up, so my generation needed to deal with the mess.

Clothing is a way of expressing ourselves. That's a big reason why I'm so interested in it. Clothing is so important for us. For me, I love choosing what to wear. It makes me feel more confident. It can perk any of us up if we're having a down day. When you understand the bigger picture of the garment industry, you realize that how your clothes are made affects the rest of the world. You have to balance the two: the joy of clothing you love and the ethics of the industry.

There's a lot of work that goes into my blog and it's even more time-consuming when you're doing it for a greater purpose. Once you build up an audience and they engage with you, you have to realize the influence you have on people. I find it important to use social media because it can be so powerful to use these platforms. It has taken me more than six years to get to where I am. My following has built up gradually. It's important that people wanting to start blogging know that it does take time.

There is a lot of pressure on teenagers to look a certain way. When I didn't know as much as I do now, I would shop in fast fashion stores. I went through a time of loving ASOS. I loved the free delivery and the fact that I could so easily buy something new and exciting to wear. Because I was only a teen and didn't have much budget, I would order the cheapest stuff because there was a thrill that came with it. Now that I know the consequences I find it harder to relate to people who still do that – someone who says, 'I only want new things.' The last clothing item I bought was a blouse from a charity shop and I love it.

I know in my gut I'm doing the right thing. I know I don't have loads of pairs of shoes or the latest 'it' items in the way that nearly everyone does, but I also know I wouldn't change.

Even after educating myself on the industry and its dark sides, I still want eventually to go into design. I have dreams of being part of the industry and making sure there are as few negative consequences for the environment and for people as possible.

Obviously, most young people feel they need to fit in with everyone else, but once you are past that barrier you become freer. You can play around with what you wear and use it to express yourself. It's such a great tool. It gives you a different mindset about the clothes themselves.

I get so much encouragement from the comments on my blog. My followers sound so sincere. They tell me that they have stopped shopping from a certain brand and that they are trying to think more consciously. When I write about being self-confident and being myself, people tell me they can relate to that and connect with that.

Personally, I feel most confident when I'm wearing chunky heels and a backpack. I worked this out recently. I feel really strong. I think it's like armour. These things are different for everyone. You can be depressed, and colourful clothes can be what helps you. Other people need to feel comfy and that's what makes them feel better. While I'm not promoting shopping, I know it can lift you up. Once I was listening to the Guilty Feminist podcast and one woman on the panel said she suffered from depression. She said she hadn't been feeling so great, so she went and bought a pair of earrings, and that was just enough to get her to the recording.

Slogan tee-shirts are another way of expressing ourselves and our beliefs, but it's important that they don't toe the line of hypocrisy – for example, we shouldn't be promoting feminist slogans if the garment has been made unethically.

When I was a younger, I would go shopping with my sister and I have great memories of that and the fun time we had. You can still have that feeling when you shop alternatively. There is a stigma around charity shops, but I find them just as fun.

No one person has the right to say 'You shouldn't be wearing that' or 'You shouldn't be doing that.' Everyone has the choice to do what they want to do, and that's the way it should be, but the media play a big role in how we are portrayed. There is a pressure on young women to look a certain way. I have a privileged perspective on that because I'm genetically very slim. For most people, I'm the ideal, so I have to bear that in mind when I discuss these issues. It's important to make space for people who feel excluded by the media so that they can talk about these things.

The good thing with my generation is that we are more open-minded, but that doesn't mean that there are enough people putting ideas into action. It takes a lot to stand up and say, 'I'm going to work on this.' On the other hand, yesterday I received an Instagram message from someone I used to go to school with, asking, 'Can you recommend me some ethical brands?' I was so pleased. I do think our generation is thinking about this more. We are more aware that there is so much we can learn and so much we must do. We have voices, you just need to listen.

TOLMEIA

@tollydollyposh

www.tollydollyposhfashion.com

"When you understand the bigger picture of the garment industry, you realize that how your clothes are made affects the rest of the world. It takes a lot to stand up and say, 'I'm going to work on this.'"

ANAHIT,

16, Kapan, Armenia

"Everyone thought that only an adult English teacher could teach. I'm so happy I could help them learn."

I have displayed a special love and interest in the English language since I was a little girl. It was always my favourite subject and I dreamed of becoming an English teacher. I don't know why I loved it so much, but I did, and I persevered with learning it with my whole love and passion. In my home town there were other students passing English at school, but their interest wasn't as strong.

Try as I could, I was unable to understand my love of English. I didn't even have anyone in my family who liked speaking it as I did. I spent my early years trying to find people to practise speaking with. Sometimes random tourists came to my small town: we have fantastic nature which brings visitors. So, when I was still 11, I would wake up early in the morning and go to the tourists' favourite places and wait for them there. If any arrived, I would start chatting, talking to them about their countries, telling them about my country and my town, and show them the places that sightseers visit. The tourists would say, 'Your English is so good, keep on practising,' which really encouraged me.

As the years passed, I didn't lose my devotion to the language. I knew there was an American Corner in my town where American volunteers would gather and hold discussions in English. They would chiefly talk about American culture and history. I started attending every meeting held there. I would learn new words, improve my pronunciation, explore the culture and feel a bit closer to the language. I attended seminars, lessons and meetings in American Corner for more than five years. I asked them to provide lessons and courses for children of my age and they did.

After working hard and practising a lot, I realized I could add another element to my love of English: volunteering.

I came up with the idea of creating my own English club for kids. I knew that for many of us in Armenia, learning English can be the key to brighter future. Armenians say, 'You can be as many humans, as many languages you speak.'

I was 14 and remembered how hard it was for me to find ways to practise and improve my English. Now I had helped to create a bridge to connect some of the local children with the language. I opened my own club and called it 'Let's Speak English'. On the first day I didn't know if anyone would attend. I was worried that no one would show up. I couldn't believe it when many children started attending. There were ten students in my first lesson. Day by day their number was increasing, and I was so excited to see them. Most of them were studying at 6th or 7th grade at school, so they were 12–13 years old – one or two years younger than me. They were truly interested in learning.

No one had ever seen a 14-year-old girl teaching English to other kids. Everyone thought that only an adult English teacher could teach, someone with higher education and work experience, but I knew I could help them learn. I'm so happy I could break that stereotype. I wouldn't be like a teacher but like an old friend who could correct their mistakes without a red pen, just with a few gentle comments. It had been such a struggle for me to get more English education and that's why I was so motivated to help all these children.

One of the American volunteers in Armenia was a 58-year-old woman who used to say to me, 'Girl, you have a lot to achieve.

Just keep on going and trying.' She was the best volunteer I had ever seen. She really inspired me.

Three years later I am still volunteering and teaching kids English. My childhood dream came true even earlier than I could have imagined. Every time the kids came up to me after the lessons and said, 'Thank you, we want to say that we love you very much,' I feel as if I had been paid in gold coins. These students were the best achievements of mine.

I am a positive person; I am thankful for the world. I see how the sun shines, how the snow falls, and I feel a part of this planet. Doing something good for the world, such as volunteering, makes me smile; it makes me feel good and happy. When I fail, my failures become the reason I want to improve myself. This allows you to feel pleased with failures because you can turn them into achievements.

Teenage years are the best years to grow in this way. Teenagers are the pillars of the world and I'm not saying this because I'm a teenager; I'll say this even when I have grandchildren. You can never be as creative and captivating as teens are. You can never love and hate life together as strongly as we do. Other people can never understand why we want to cry and to smile, how we can be happy and sad in one minute. We are changeable, but as a teenager I want to say that this is the cycle of life. It happens because we appreciate everything differently. We are working on ourselves and creating our individuality. We create our hobbies and interests; we gain experience in different situations; we get to know new friends. All these steps create us as an individual. We can't make these changes when we are very old or very young. We are creating our personality with our own values. We can become the person we want to see when we are 60.

ANAHIT

https://www.youtube.com/channel/UCpisLVIiFU66RlhdwGbYuDQ/featured?view_as=subscriber

"My failures become the reason I want to improve myself. This allows you to feel pleased with failures because you can turn them into achievements."

LILY,

**14, Huddersfield,
England**

"I want to do robotics after school. I'm going to create robots who can do the talking for autistic people and help them with social situations. I could have one on my shoulder now going, 'I'm not talking right now.'"

Talking to people my age was never easy for me. I thought the problem was them. It was my teacher who said when I was in year 4* that she thought I had Asperger's.

If I was in loud places, sometimes I'd run off. I'd find the noise chaotic and it hurt my ears. I struggled to make friends and that carried on as I got older, and I still do. I felt different because other people were obsessed with what was popular and I didn't give two hoots about that sometimes. Some of those things I actually care about, like pop music that sounds like someone dragging fingernails down a blackboard.

Over the years I've had to learn that other people were not interested in what I am interested in. A hard lesson to learn.

At primary school I made a lot of animal noises. I was trying to pretend I wasn't quirky, but it makes life harder when you're trying to be something you're not. The others would walk away or hiss back at me and still move away. People always moved away.

Some schools would refuse to acknowledge that I was 'different' (their words, not mine) in any way. They thought I was behaving like an autistic person on purpose, just to annoy people. In maths lessons I would tell them a different way to do the sums, but they saw that as disrespectful. They thought I was caricaturing the teacher. I was just saying that in their way you have to write everything down; in my way, you did everything in your head.

I changed to go to another primary school that was better. In fact, they were amazing! The support was amazing, and the teachers were crazier than the children (but in a good way). It was

---

*　Ages 8–9.

nice, and we learned lots. Then I went to another new school and they really weren't very good with my autism at all. I got the impression that when the teacher was telling me that I was autistic, she meant that I was stupid. They were very patronizing in the way that they spoke.

I remember one time that this child started poking fun at me. I shouted at him for doing this and they told him to apologize 'because Lily doesn't always understand social interactions'. You see – patronizing.

I do have some friends, people who can put up with me for long periods of time. Everyone needs a friend, someone they feel comfortable talking to. There's safety in numbers. There's bullying in nearly every school I have been to, which is quite a few, but most of the time nothing happens after you've reported it, which seems a bit like a pointless system to me.

Some things about school are OK. I'm really good at maths; I'm not so good at physics but quite good at science. I'm all right at some parts of English. I can write stories but I'm not so good at writing letters. I have to think about why the writer's done this instead of doing that and I'm not good at understanding motivation. At a dance night I ended up shaking, clinging on to my friend for dear life. A lot of the people at the dance were being very mean, and the overwhelming music left me in that state. Sensory overload from loud noise is often like that, and I also didn't understand what was expected of me in that environment. The teachers told me to pull myself together.

Quite a few times I have needed some peace, alone time, and when people have tried to make me feel better, they usually end up with their head bitten off. I see now that I was being very rude to them, but I was too upset to think about it then. I now wear ear defenders to keep me calm, and to dampen the sound and reduce the overall amount of level of sensory input. School lets me wear them because I was sitting in a corner, rocking, with my hands over my ears.

I like automation and machines. That new automated ordering system in McDonalds: my mum hates it and I love it. Machines don't judge you. I go to a club where you go and program robots and

sometimes they let you build robots. I want to do robotics after school. This is going to be my ticket to take over the world. World domination is my plan! All hail Supreme Leader Emperor Lily! I'm going to create robots who can do the talking for autistic people and help them with social situations. I could have one on my shoulder now, going, 'I'm not talking right now.' This would stop me having to talk to people I don't know, or don't want to talk to, or it will stop people from trying to talking to me when I need a moment, so their heads don't get bitten off.

People have quite a few disabilities involving speech: pronounced speech impediments or stammering that is really difficult for them. My robot could help them too. Some people who physically can't speak have to carry a text-to-speech device, but that's a huge piece of equipment to carry around with them. My robot will be small, compact.

I want to influence society. Society likes to kid itself into thinking it is quite accepting, but it's not. I'm putting my foot down. This is who I am. One of my friends has another way of doing this. She has a motorized wheelchair, and if she doesn't like you, she will run over your foot. She puts her foot down by using her feet to run over your feet. To me, it's funny.

LILY

> "Society likes to kid itself into thinking it is quite accepting, but it's not. I'm putting my foot down. This is who I am."

6...

TURNING MY
LIFE AROUND

JENIFFER,

21, Mangochi, Malawi

"I was tricked into marriage at 14 and dropped out of school. I went back and told everyone that education is our future."

When I was 14, I agreed to get married to an older man, a businessman. He was 30, so a lot older than me, but I was very happy with the decision. I am from a poor family and I thought my future would be with him.

It was peer pressure from my friends at school that convinced me to get married. In my early teens, most of my friends were already married. Those who were not married were already having sexual partners. This is not what I had wanted and my mother made time to give me advice against the marriage, but after listening to my friends I chose not to hear her.

I dropped out of school and planned the wedding myself. It was beautiful. All my relatives and my husband's relatives were there. My husband gave me gifts and called me romantic names, which I loved.

Two days before the wedding, my husband had told me he already had a wife and child. I accepted this because my husband promised me he would divorce his first wife. I believed because of my tender age that I could compete with the first wife. His first wife was shocked when she found out about me because she was expecting her second child.

I knew I was looking pretty and attractive to my husband. I thought this meant my husband would be caring and would be looking after me all the time. To me, this was a good match and I was satisfied. I felt that dropping out of school had been a good decision because my future would be secure.

However, my husband failed to support me as he had agreed. He also failed to divorce his first wife, who would verbally abuse me, calling me a prostitute, a bar girl and other bad names to make me feel bad for snatching her husband. I felt angry and uncomfortable. In the first days, my husband protected me, but this didn't last long. Soon he was using his power to force me to have sex with him. He was unfaithful to me and was sleeping in the house just two days a week.

Luckily, I did not get pregnant, but I found myself in a nightmare situation and I didn't know what to do. I felt betrayed and at a loss. I had thought I had everything I wanted in life. Now I knew I had to escape.

At 16 I heard about a campaign run by the Malawi Girl Guides Association Officials at an open day in my area. This gave girls who had dropped out of school a second chance to go back. When I learned about this, I made the decision to go back to school. It was a powerful moment for me. My mother was on my side. She helped me go forward and not reverse my decision. My husband knew what I was doing and he didn't try to stop me.

The day I walked back into school was a happy one. From that day I focused on my studies to achieve my goal of a better life. I had one more problem, which was an unsafe, two-hour journey walking to school, but the Girl Guides gave me and the other girls returning to school a bicycle, paid for by the United Nations Population Fund and its Joint Program on Adolescent Girls, which minimized the problem. A huge relief.

I had just been away from school for a year. I felt shy when I returned because the others were calling me bad names. As time went on, I manage to cope. I found my voice and stood up for myself. I started sharing my story for other girls to hear.

Then I had the chance to go to a special event in Washington, DC, the Girl Up Leadership Summit, which was facilitated by the United Nations Population Fund and aimed at keeping girls in school. This was my chance to share my story in front of more people. I felt powerful travelling abroad. It motivated me. It was a true privilege. I didn't want other girls to be misled into making bad decisions and listening to stories that weren't true, and I knew I could help stop them. In Washington I talked to around 250 girls in school and 50 out of school. I was driven to keep them away from the situation I had been in, so that took away my fear of speaking.

It was painful hearing about other girls' experiences, but this made me even more clear that I was doing the right thing. My call was for abstinence during the school years. I was showing the girls that they had other opportunities. I wanted to prevent unhappy early marriages and teen pregnancies.

Through abstinence we can prevent diseases like HIV and AIDS, and other STIs, as well as pregnancies. This can help girls achieve their set goals in life. I feel I am a good mentor for girls. I use different skills like songs, role play and panel discussion, as well as talking through personal experiences. I also encourage girls if they are sexually active to use health services and condoms.

At least eight girls have left their marriages after listening to me. One was made pregnant in her early teens and her husband left her without any help at all. After her delivery she went back to school and has taken her exams this year. Other girls were tricked into marriage; their husbands did not support them and treated them badly even though they have children. Like me, they did not give up on themselves.

When I leave school, I want to be a nurse or a soldier. It is so important for teenagers to do what feels right for them, and not give in to what others expect. The best way we can do this is by concentrating on our strengths which will help us prosper. We must stop looking down on ourselves.

In Malawi, life is easier for men than women. Most of the time women are let down by men. Women need to fight for what is fair for themselves.

My advice to girls is to set their goals and do all they can to focus on achieving them. Education is the key to our future life.

JENIFFER

Malawi Girl Guides Association (MAGGA)

@GirlGuidesMw

www.magga.org

Photograph of Jeniffer by the United Nations Foundation

"The day I walked back into school was a happy one. I found my voice and stood up for myself. I started sharing my story for other girls to hear."

AMARNI,

17, London, England

"I made the decision to walk away from trouble. One of my objectives is to help people in my situation who feel lost. I want to shine the light on people for the positive things they do."

Older people say things that young people don't agree with. Sometimes we don't get the chance to have a voice ourselves. On the news they've said that trap music is one of the leading causes of knife crime. I don't agree with that, even though the words do talk about killing people.

If we had our own podcast station, we could reply, we could say how we see things. If we had our say, this could make a difference. Sometimes music does give you the wrong way to go but sometimes, instead of taking something to the level of violence, the music is a way of saying, 'This is how I feel.' We can relate to the words and it calms us down.

I lead the music department here at the Copenhagen Youth Project. I make sure the studio is kept clean and presentable, but I've got plans to jazz it up. I want it to look exciting and relaxed at the same time. My idea is that we can get paint and brushes and do it ourselves.

I make sure the young people at the project have a safe place to make the music they want. We can help them with UK rap and Afrobeats. My end goal is to make a radio show here, get some cameras, get it all kitted up, get some famous people down. I'd like to get us on the news so more and more people know about what we're doing.

I'd like the chance to talk about youth culture and discuss youth issues. There's quite an atmosphere in here when there's a lot of people filling the place. We want to get enough music out and our voices out there too.

Music is central to who I am. I was given my first drum kit when I was 9 or 10: half of a Yamaha kit, passed down from my cousin.

It meant a lot to me; it helped me deal with a lot of frustration and anger and I played to relieve the stress.

The other thing that helped me was my primary school headteacher who got me a scholarship for five years with Lewisham Music Services; then this got extended for two more. This made quite a difference: what was given to me compared with what was given to others. Friends I have grown up with from primary school don't do anything now. When I walk past them, I say, 'I'm working.' I tell them what I'm doing, and they say, 'I'm still on the road.' When I was younger, I used to find that kind of life cool, but now I've seen what it does to people living outside the law: not just the children but also mothers, fathers, sisters, brothers. It's not good. You don't want to be in that situation. The thing that my headteacher did, it has changed my life and I think if only they could have done that for more people.

A lot of people were not in my corner. Some teachers didn't like me. I was a cheeky boy. They were out to make it worse, to make sure I got into trouble, but some teachers were saying, 'We are not going to highlight that behaviour. You are good at music: we will highlight that.'

In secondary school I started hanging round with the wrong people. There was a Sainsbury's next to our school. We used to shoplift and do stupid things. In Lewisham, if you're in a group, they are called batches. If you're in a batch and you're targeted by another group, they would fight you or try to rob you.

I was with three people from my batch and this guy from Eltham said to me, 'If I ever catch you, I'm going to stab you up.' I called a couple of uncles to be with me and he didn't show. I was still expecting him, so I brought a knife into school halfway through year 9.* It was fear of him and fear of not being respected if I lost, but mainly fear.

I hid the knife in the roof, thinking I was being smart. I was called out of class and searched, and I said, 'There's nothing in my bag,' but they found out what I'd done on CCTV. They kicked me out, but they told me to make sure I found another school first. I moved to the north of London and found a college near my grandma.

At my old school I was one of the top guys, not the leader of a gang but people older than me respected me. It felt cool and it got to my head until I saw how much trouble came with it. There are only two ways you will end up with trouble – in prison or dead. So many times, I didn't end up dead. My mum says the angels are protecting me.

When I went to the college, every day people would be waiting outside with knives. I knew by then I didn't want trouble. I would stay after hours in the music department. At college, they were thinking I was going to be a bad person, but I was the opposite and worked hard. They helped me move school to a place that

---

* Ages 13–14.

felt safer. Again, I was pre-judged a lot by the teachers. They expected me to be troublesome, always getting into fights. Some of my friends there were hanging round with bad people. One guy and his brother started getting into a gang and asked me to come out with them. The teachers pulled me in and said you don't want to be hanging round with them and I avoided them for as long as I could.

Then one guy at school pushed me down the stairs. I told him, 'I'm not going to fight you.' He was tall and I'm quite short. In the corridor he came up to me again and started on my friends. I pushed him and asked him what's wrong. I said, 'Let's talk.' I think saying that surprised him – I surprised myself.

Some teachers thought I wasn't as bad as the others; others said I was going to be bad when I was older. I would get pulled out of lessons for stupid things. I tried so hard; I went to special classes to make teachers see that I'm not really this guy you think I am. Props to the school, the policy on behaviour was really strict.

By chance I have gone through what I have gone through and I have made it. To survive you don't have to be a Perfect Peter, but if your friends are going to watch a fight and you know one of the people there will have a knife or if it's a rival fight, just go home. That decision to go home could save your life. Or save someone else's life. Find another direction.

Now, so many people come up to me in north London with knives, going, 'Where are you from?' I act like I'm a tourist. I say, 'I'm not from round here; just coming up to you, friend,' and they say, 'Cool.'

I have seen my grandma frightened for her life because my uncle has gone out and not come back for two days. People come into her house to find him, come to where she sleeps, and she doesn't know where he is. It should make you think, 'Is it worth it?' He's made a good decision to move away and start another life.

Working here has helped me a lot. One of my objectives is to help people in my situation who feel lost. I have a friend who was good at football. People said to him. 'Do this with your football, do that with your football,' but he never did. We went to this London martial arts place together and we both shone, and they wanted to take us further, but he didn't show up. We are both 17 now. I ask him, 'What are you doing?' and he said, 'I don't know.'

I got him a job in the supermarket where I work. The manager wasn't happy that it took him five days to fill in the application. Once there, he wasn't showing no effort. I told him, 'It's your life,' but you can't force someone to do it. You can't push it. It sounds harsh but sometimes you have to learn and go through something and then that thing that will help you in life will click.

The Copenhagen Youth Centre has given so many people chances, so many opportunities, including me. One guy came here for football; now he's a successful actor. I've had the opportunity, the freedom, to do what I want to do. It makes me learn. This place, it's like a machine. You come in and they find out how to help. If something doesn't work out, you start again. You find a way.

A lot of people don't like to listen; I don't either, but I have worked on it. In my work here, I want to shine the light on people for the positive things they do. It would be great if as well as saying 'There's been four deaths,' the news would say, 'And this person has got a record deal.' 'This person died, this person got stabbed, but this guy has made a track and it's gone viral.' It's hard because there are a lot of obstacles to succeeding in this business, but there are also a lot of chances.

AMARNI

"One guy at school pushed me down the stairs. I told him, 'I'm not going to fight you.' I said, 'Let's talk.' I think saying that surprised him. I surprised myself."

HAPPY D,

19, Glasgow, Scotland

"I thought I would be someone who would never learn to read. I thought I had a bad brain. Now I am slowly reading books."

At primary school, the teachers didn't realize I couldn't read. When I tried, the letters were blurred and moving on the page. When I was 9, one of them saw that I wasn't coping and said something was wrong with my eyes. I went to get them checked and they gave me coloured glasses. I was dyslexic and they realized I couldn't cope with looking at things in black and white.

Then I went to high school where they didn't know what to do with me. They didn't bother with me. They asked me to run messages or told me to sit by myself and draw.

I was getting bullied, and when I told the teachers, they just said, 'Don't let them bully you.' I had one friend there and the teachers told her not to hang about with me because people were bullying me. So I was completely by myself. The others would say things like 'Haha, he's got blue glasses.' They'd call me names and barge into me. The worst thing was that when they barged into me on the way to lunch, I fell down and hurt my knee, and they'd laugh, saying I'd fallen down because I was blind.

I felt completely by myself. I didn't know what to do. I was scared in case telling my mum would make it worse. It was the worst time in my life.

I tried very hard to read, but they'd take the books away before I could manage. I thought I would be someone who would never learn to read, that maybe there was something wrong with my eyes or that I had a bad brain. When I was alone with no one to talk to, I felt like an outcast.

Finally, I told my mum what was happening, and she fought for me to go to an additional support school. This really helped me.

The teachers there were a lot better; it was like they really cared about me and the others there. Also it was easier to make friends.

I started getting involved in drama and felt as if this was my calling as I liked performing and making people laugh. One teacher in particular really helped to guide me through my emotions and he encouraged me to use drama as a platform to express myself. When I was more confident with my reading, they gave me a part in the play *Aladdin*. I took the script home and I couldn't believe I was going to be the genie. A main part. It was like being in a different world. I really got into character and didn't take myself too seriously. It was so good to see people laugh with me and not at me. It kind of gave me some inner hope.

At this school there was also a reading tool called 'Toe by Toe' that helped improve my reading at a relaxed pace. At first I didn't progress, but when I focused and the teachers were focusing, explaining and taking it nice and slow, this really helped.

The change in me happened gradually but the new school was a key factor. The encouraging and non-judgemental culture put me at ease. I could see that life could be fun, exciting and positive. I also realized that humour could be a great tool for forging friendships and I knew I was good at making people laugh. One of the teachers, Mr Ray, helped bring my confidence right up. I told him what had happened at my last school and he said, 'Look at you now. See how far you have come.'

In the new school I had friends. If I was struggling, I would ask for help. I didn't have to sit by myself. By 13 or 14, I began to read. I wasn't very good, but I was beginning to learn and to express myself. The teachers really helped me.

Now I am slowly reading books. I would say to anyone with dyslexia that you will get the hang of it, and if you are struggling, there are always people who will help you.

If you knew me before and you saw me now, you wouldn't recognize me. When you realized it was me, you would go, 'Wow'. In the past I would keep quiet and hope no one would bully me; I was scared I would do something wrong and they would say I was stupid. Now I will be on that stage, performing. My life is transformed.

I've realized that as you get older you begin to find what you are good at. You can stand your ground more. I can stand up and be proud of who I am. I learned that I can make friends; I can make them happy and make myself happy. My mum says I never talked, I never ever talked, and now I don't shut up!

I also worked with a mentor at the organization Move On who helped me to try new things. We learned how to play the guitar together and he'd take me to a pool hall, the cinema and for a bite to eat. We also went to a place called Megabytes where we could meet other young people and play computer games. My mentor was like a sounding board. I could tell him anything and he listened. Now I'm at college and life is going so well.

I think teenage years can be difficult as there are all sorts of things happening like hormonal and emotional changes. On the other hand, it's a good time to identify other skills and abilities – like acting for me.

I'm not sure if I am someone who can motivate others, but I do think that good things can come from bad. Because of my own experiences, I tend not to be judgemental and I can often pick up when others aren't feeling great. Young people should never give up. Focus on the positive people in your life, like family or folk in school. These are the people who helped me and encouraged me to push myself out of my comfort zone. They inspired me to give it a go. Look at areas of your life you can change and believe in yourself.

HAPPY D

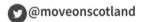 @moveonscotland

"Teenage years are a good time to identify other skills and abilities — like acting for me."

MOHAMMED,*

18, London, England

"I turned away from my religion and lost connection with my family but I've found a new life, campaigning against radicalisation and forced marriage."

---

* Name has been changed.

Although I was born into a Muslim background, when I was 16 I decided I didn't want to be a part of it. At school we were learning about different religious topics and I started to question things. I suppose you could say I had an identity crisis. I ended up realizing that since the beginning of my life I had never asked the questions I had wanted to ask. That made me think I had never been given a choice.

Since then, for the past two years, I have struggled. I feel like I have been pretending to be someone I'm not. It's been draining. I feel I have lost the connection with my family because my parents are of a different generation. I still have to go home and be somewhere I don't fit in, but when I'm not at home I'm growing a new life, a different life.

In college I've found some people I can confide in and they've been trying to help me cope with my identity crisis. For a while I was depressed and wasn't doing anything with my life, but now I've got involved in a charity and do outreach work for them and this has changed me. I go into schools and speak to teachers, professionals and kids there about extremist behaviour: about female genital mutilation (FGM); grooming boys and girls for radicalization; honour-based violence; and forced marriage. These are not everyday issues but I'm against them all. I want to help out to make sure these things don't happen. When I think of these issues, I think, 'This could be a friend of mine affected or one of my cousins.' This is why I want to get as involved as possible. I want people who are good not to suffer.

If my parents knew what I was doing, the family's reputation would be affected. There would be dishonour. For me, I don't care.

I want to get out as soon as possible. For them, it would be shame. For me, what I'm doing is so important. I am tackling the extremes of religion, traditions and culture. For many people it would be dishonourable to talk about FGM, but we need more people to know about this. We need as many young people as possible to have a voice and stand up for what we believe is right. Working for the charity offers me a platform to fight against the gravity of what's been happening.

My voluntary work is helping me to explore my new life. It allows me to see how young people can hear and speak the message. It's given me a place to think for myself. It helps me make my own life and my own journey. I won't let anyone else make my choices.

MOHAMMED

"We need as many young people as possible to have a voice and stand up for what we believe is right."

CORIE,

14, Merthyr Tydfil, Wales

"At primary school I was bullied and no one saw me as a suitable friend. On my first day of high school I realized I had a clean slate. I vowed my life would be different."

When I was in primary school I was bullied, and I never had the chance to make friends. No one wanted to talk to me. No one saw me as a suitable friend. There were so many preconceptions about me and what I was like. I would get angry and kick off and still no one wanted to talk to me. My reputation got lower.

Looking back, I think this was mostly because of my interests, as I love trains, and my autism. I think they may have made a bad assumption – that I was childish and not to be taken seriously.

They would find something that would annoy me and keep on doing it. Constantly. Every time they did this, I felt like I was being exploited. I was very lonely. I once listened to the conversations of a group who were in the year below me and I think they were saying I was weak.

When I was 11 and came to secondary school, the other kids who came from my primary to this school were kids who didn't bother me. A lot of people find secondary school harder than primary, but, oddly, I made my first friend on my first day at this school. I was standing in a queue and I looked behind me and thought, 'I want to make friends with that kid.' I wanted my life in this school to be different. We had a tour of the school and I ended up talking to him. I thought he was different from the others. We ended up making friends.

Making my first friend definitely raised my confidence. Now, every time I make a friend, I run home and tell my mum that I've made a friend and what their name is.

I think when I first walked through the gates of this school, I realized people didn't know me. This meant they couldn't make any assumptions about me. I had a clean slate. I'm not really good at first impressions but this time I got it right. I realized that people could be so different and so similar at the same time. People can be mean, and people can be nice. At secondary school I could see this.

When you're being bullied and you have no friends, people always tell you that things will get better. Well, I can tell you that eventually they will. I can also tell you that, as well as that, your past will make you stronger. I found that because of what I had been through I had developed a resistance to insults. I think I had so many insults I became a bit numb to them. Even now, if someone is mean, my friends will get angry on my behalf, but I will take the insult as a joke or even as a compliment – that they have noticed me and are commenting on me. I don't care anymore. Only certain things that people say tick me off – if it's something I'm passionate about. Mostly, I feel angry when they bring up autism and they say something that they think is true. I want to tell them no, they're wrong, but I also know that because they are wrong, what they are saying doesn't apply to me so there's no way I can really be affected.

Having friends has made life easier. No question. One of the reasons I have developed this inner strength is because I have more support.

Because of my experiences, I have developed lots of ideas about how to run schools in a better way. I would have specific education programmes for every student, especially for the ones who misbehave. For those students, if information is delivered to them in the wrong way, they don't see the need to listen. Then they carry along other people who also don't want to learn with them.

I'd also have a lesson a day or a lesson a week just talking to a teacher, building a relationship with them. The teacher could listen and help, and this would relieve some of your feelings.

Also, to help relieve students of stress, I'd get rid of tests and the anxiety that comes with them. With tests, if you get a certain amount wrong and have to redo the whole thing, that's what's in the back of your mind when you're doing the next test and it stops you from getting the marks you could get.

In primary school, I felt as if I didn't have much to contribute. I would rather work by myself as there was no point me being in a group. Here, there is a point being in a group because I have friends. I have confidence that I know I will be listened to and can contribute, so I come up with ideas that can make a difference.

Most people think coming up with ideas to make changes is cheesy. They don't realize that if things are done differently, this can be inspirational. School is made for extroverts, but the people who really need help are the introverts. There is nothing for us here. Everything is about being socialized, talking and having fun. I'm proud of being an introvert. I know that even if you don't socialize, you can be a good person. You can learn. You can make friends. You can do things the way you do them. You can make change happen.

CORIE

"I'm proud of being an introvert. I know that even if you don't socialize, you can be a good person. You can make friends."

NINA,

22, Sheffield, England

"Mum died when I was 14. I struggled with anorexia but even during my most desolate times, I still felt her love somewhere deep inside."

Mum didn't ever want me to be hurt so she protected me from what was happening during her struggle with cancer. I wouldn't visit her in hospital because I was in denial, and she didn't force me to. I found out she was dying four days before she died. I was only 14.

Some of us are brought up to believe that kids are vulnerable and fragile and that adults know it all. The truth is that kids know and understand a lot more than people often give them credit for and we always carry the vulnerability of children within our hearts, whether we are 8 or 80.

Looking back, during my mum's illness I was full of denial and suppressed emotion which I expressed through self-destruction and anger. I remember my mum came home from hospital once. Seeing her really unwell was really rough and I didn't know how to process all the conflicting emotions her illness was causing me. I remember shouting at her about some pyjamas. Of course, it wasn't actually about the pyjamas.

She said to me, 'I know you're angry.' I said I wasn't, but I knew I was. Thinking about it now, I think I was also extremely stressed about what would happen to me emotionally and practically if my best friend and my whole world died, while trying to not accept that this was a possibility.

The last time I saw Mum, she was writhing in pain. She died the next day and I went into foster care three weeks later.

My anorexia started while Mum was ill, when I was around 12. Restricting what I ate somehow gave me a false sense of control over my mum's illness. For a few years I was dealing with my illness and was on a very firm road to recovery, although sadly I relapsed and was sectioned when I was 16.

Looking back, it is clear that my anorexia was never about the food. It was a symptom of my depression and food became what I used to try to gain a sense of control over what was going on and what had gone in my life. For me, anorexia was an emotional illness.

During my time in hospital, I started managing my illness well enough to be allowed to go to a two-week-long Buddhist retreat. While I was there, I had a lightbulb moment and I realized I wanted to get better so I could get out of hospital. I realized that restricting food wasn't going to make me feel better, but recovery and rebuilding my life was. When I got back from hospital, I discharged myself and started attending sixth form college* three weeks later.

Experiencing so much trauma and loss at such an early age means I was pulled out of any kind of bubble of comfort that I could have lived in. This radically opened me up to the fact that even though the world can be an extremely beautiful place, there is a lot of pain and struggle here and there is a lot of work to be done to help others. I have learned to give a shit because I know that anything can affect anyone, irrespective of where you're from, and we all have a responsibility to look after one another even if the other person's struggles will never affect us personally.

I used to be an all-or-nothing person. I was the most amazing people pleaser, the saviour for everyone. Now I'm there for people in a way that doesn't damage myself. My experiences mean that I utilize the pain I experienced to try to do work that is going to make things easier for others. I worked for a charity that improves in-patient care for kids; I independently organized three mental health conferences on topics surrounding children's mental health

---

*   Sixth form college is for 16–18-year-olds.

and have given talks on the radio, at hospital clinics and at mental health events. In the future, I really want to adopt children. So many kids need love and I have so much love to give. I also know that the hardest to love need the most love. Currently, I am working for a charity providing clean water, sanitation and hygiene training in rural Kenya as a fundraising support officer.

I climbed Everest Base Camp, and there I discovered a passion for mountains. When I climb, I feel close to my mum. Even though I don't believe in the concept of people who die sitting in heaven on clouds, something about being near and above the clouds makes me feel like I am near her.

I remember my mum every day, and one of the ways that I do this is by drawing on the strength she gave me. I am lucky to have the ancestry of a lot of strong women and still today I am surrounded by many strong women. A year before my mum died, she said to me, 'You are never going to be alone. I will always be in here, in your heart,' and I know that that's true. I remember when she died, the light I had inside me didn't go out, and even during my most desolate times, I still felt her love somewhere deep inside.

What my struggles as a teenager taught me is that there is an immense amount of value in vulnerability, admitting your limits and being true to yourself. If you are struggling, source out people you trust and please, please do not be afraid to speak up. We are humans, not robots, and struggling doesn't equate to weakness. Vulnerability and admitting that things aren't OK can be our greatest strength.

NINA

"I utilize the pain I experienced to try to do work that is going to make things easier for others. My struggles as a teenager taught me that there is an immense amount of value in vulnerability and being true to yourself."

KAYDEN,

19, Glasgow, Scotland

"At 14 I went into residential care. Now I am volunteering in youth work. I know I have the inner strength to change young people's lives."

When I was 14 up until I turned 17, I was in residential care. Going into care was probably the best thing that could have happened to me at that point in my life. It gave me new opportunities and turned me into a more caring person. It was hard at the start, moving into a group home with people already in friendship groups, but as time went on it became easier.

I struggled with bullying at school because people thought it was weird that I was in care. They thought I must be a violent or bad child, but I wasn't and I'm not. I went into care because I didn't enjoy staying at home, my mum wasn't coping, and my little brother was always getting angry and punching things in the house. Going into care gave us time apart.

In care, I started getting on with my life and learning new things. I made new friends, spent time with other people, went out on trips, and had one-to-one support available at all times. I always kept myself busy, so I didn't have to think about all the bad times. Life was more positive. When I went back home after my time in care, we all got along much better.

Because of the bullying, I left school at 14 and went to college where I did childcare courses. It was the best thing I could have done. I want to be a youth worker and help other people and, whenever I got help, I watched the people who helped me and worked out the different ways they do it.

Another thing that happened when I went to college was that I showed a youth worker my music and she said it was good and that I should start performing and get some songs recorded. I rap about being in care, my personal experiences and what has happened to me in my life. I do this so that I can help other young people in the same position I was in then. I volunteer with music groups, which gives me the chance to help young people engage in positive writing, and I help them create their own raps and beats. Without that youth worker, I probably wouldn't have believed I had the ability to do what I do now. Writing music is one of the main things that's helped me – being able to express myself and having people around me I can share it with.

I know I have the inner strength to change young people's lives, especially young people who are going through difficult situations: being in care, leaving care, self-harm, alcohol and drug misuse. I enjoy having the chance to engage with young people and finding out what I can do to help their situations. I am volunteering at the moment in the youth work industry and I know I am helping change the young people's outlook on life.

If we make the changes when we're in our teens, it means things will be easier in adult life. If we don't try to change now, we won't have time when we are adults and our lives will just be the same forever. I think all teenagers should have the opportunity to be who they want to be, and if that means changing life now, that's what they should do.

There is always time for change. Just do what you feel is right. I have been where you are now, and I got through it, so you can too. Try to see the positive in a negative. It will make your life much easier.

KAYDEN

 @moveonscotland

"I want to be a youth worker and help other people. Whenever I got help, I watched the people who helped me and worked out the different ways they do it."

BEN,

23, London, England

"All my life people had been saying I was a tomboy but I knew I was more than that. My feelings ran deeper."

When I was 2 years old I remember trying to go to the toilet standing up. At 5 I was confused about being made to wear dresses and make-up: tracksuits made me so much happier. I really wanted to be able to take my top off whenever I wanted like boys could. I think I always felt that I was in the wrong body but said nothing.

My brother and I were taken away from our parents at a very young age and grew up in care. First, we went to care homes. Then, when I was 4, we went to stay with my aunt and cousins.

My aunt had four kids and we all grew up together. I was a tomboy and I wanted to be like my big brother and his mates. I wanted to wear boys' clothes and I didn't mind getting muddy. My girl cousin was the same but then, at 10 or 11, she started changing to a more feminine and girlie look and I didn't.

All my life people had been saying, 'You're just a tomboy,' but I knew I was more than that. My feelings ran deeper.

I decided to start reading up about what it was like to be trapped in a different body and, at 9, I found the courage to talk to my brother about how I felt. It was the toughest conversation I had ever had. Throughout our lives we had been together and I thought I could tell him. I took a deep breath and it all just come out, me saying I wanted to be his little brother, not his little sister.

Unfortunately, he didn't accept what I was saying. He wanted to 'fix me'. For me, this was heart-breaking. He was unable to accept who I was.

After this I felt I should keep quiet. I knew being called 'she' pronouns wasn't right for me, but it seemed safer to go back into the closet.

At 11, I went to a Church of England high school. I now had more confidence and asked the teachers to call me 'he' and to use the name 'Ben', but being gay and trans didn't go well. I was bullied for being different to the other girls as I didn't fit into their world, but the students handled it better than the teachers. I was treated differently to everyone because I wanted to be who I am. I cut my hair short and was put in detention for this. I even had one teacher say, 'Are you sure you're not just a tomboy – you had a boyfriend.' So much frustration and anger come from this. I went through periods of self-harm, cutting myself, when I thought it was better to hurt myself as everyone else was hurting me. I was addicted to this for a few years and the low moods, depression and anxiety started.

What made things so much better was that one of the teachers was fighting my corner. He was saying to his colleagues, 'If this is what he wants, we should try to make him happy. When he's in class why can't we refer to him as Ben?' Knowing I had one person fighting my corner made so much difference. I still keep in touch with that teacher now. He even helped to tell my aunt, calling her one evening to discuss what was happening with me. He showed me an article in the newspaper about two friends who went to different high schools who met up later in life and one had transitioned. He really went the extra mile.

I remember the exact moment when my aunt took his phone call. I thought, 'It's all going to kick off now,' but it didn't. She told me afterwards she wondered if what was going on with me might be more than me wanting to wear boys' clothes, but said she hadn't wanted to put ideas into my mind.

My nan, who I am very close to, was in her 70s then and, for that generation, this was something that wasn't spoken of. It was definitely a struggle for her to understand.

When I found the Gender Intelligence charity this encouraged me to come out completely at 13. There, they gave me support when others had turned their back. I had to hide letters from the gender clinic I went to and was unable to take puberty blockers as my aunt wouldn't agree to this and I needed permission from my guardian. If she had agreed, my life would have been much so much easier. I would never have had to experience periods, my breasts wouldn't have grown and I wouldn't have needed surgery.

Finally when I was 19 and an adult, I was allowed to make my own decisions. It was too late for me to block my female hormones but I was able to start taking the male hormone testosterone. From here I felt I could be myself. I was accepted as a boy at college. My facial hair started to grow; my voice became deeper and at 21 I had the surgery I had been waiting for.

As a person I have always had the mindset, 'I can be more me. I can be happier.' When I no longer suffered with gender dysphoria – my gender was no longer different from the sex I had been seen to have – my life changed. I felt the way I should feel; I had my identity; I was who I knew I was. I was someone who had gone through so much and this has allowed me to help others figure out how they wanted their lives to go. Hopefully they won't face as many challenges as I have been through.

Quicker intervention and more understanding would mean they can live without the anxiety that gender dysphoria brings.

Nowadays people are coming out a lot younger. When I came out I thought I was the only one. There are more role models now. There's more in the media. In the past we held back for different reasons. Sometimes we feared going against our families, sometimes our religion. What's more important, this or our happiness? It's a dilemma.

I'm someone with a strong mind. If I'm set on something, that's it. I am not someone who follows in other people's footsteps.

My aunt has come round at lot more since she's seen the changes and she's seen how much happier I am. I never lost her and that's important to me. My nan is calling me Ben and saying 'he'. She's not completely on board but she's getting there. She knows if I hadn't transitioned I wouldn't be so content.

I have a good life. You do lose people on the way but you also gain people.

For a long time I was concerned I would end up alone. Now I have a wonderful partner and I have a great job as an activity leader. One of the most important things I do is give talks to schools. I give the talks I wish I'd heard when I was young. I always say, 'Take small steps. Don't rush anything. What's great is to have one or two people you know you can talk to and know you can trust. Tell them how you're feeling, see how they take it, and go from there.'

'Please don't give up. I know it's hard but stay strong.'

In the trans world, there are always going to be barriers. What's important is getting the support you need. Families do come around eventually; it just takes time. Changing your gender affects everyone, but if you only worry about what other people think, you forget to focus on your happiness. If they love you, people do want to see you happy. You can make decisions that bring distance but down the line these same decisions can make you closer again.

I know that if I had just been born a boy my life would have been easier but I wouldn't have had the experiences I have had. I wouldn't be able to influence today's generation. Everything I have been through has meant that I met my partner; I have met the friends I have now. Going through the challenges has made me the person I am.

BEN

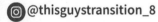 @thisguystransition_8

self_made_boy_8

> "I give talks to schools — the talks I wish I'd heard when I was young."

7...

HELPING OTHERS

WILL,

15, London, England

"I knew so much about prostate cancer and knew if we could convince even one man to get checked and save just one life, we would have done our job."

Everyone was celebrating on the opening day of the London 2012 Olympics, apart from my family. It was the day my dad was diagnosed with prostate cancer.

Dad was relatively young; he was in his late forties, so under the age bracket usually affected. He had a manual job, so if he had a pain, he would decide it was because of his work. In a way, he had been almost self-diagnosing. I know now that if you have any symptoms, you have to get them checked out. The only way cancer can be caught early is by going to your GP.

The diagnosis and Dad's illness were devastating for my family. Our whole life was turned on its head. It was totally unexpected. I was 11 and I knew my granddad and my nan well. I thought my mum and dad would be around till their late 80s, just like them. When I realized how advanced the cancer was, it hit me that I wouldn't have my dad for many years of my life. It was an indescribable shock.

At the time of diagnosis, I think I didn't really understand the complexity of the disease. I had never heard of it and I was so young. I love my dad and he was my idol. It was unbelievable that this would happen to him. It was impossible to imagine life without him.

The small proportion of my life that I had with Dad is something I'll always remember. That is a big positive for me. I spent almost every day of my life with him. Dad was the caretaker in my school, so I went into work with him even in the holidays. During term time I went in early with him and came home late when he finished work. At the time it didn't seem a big thing, but now it's something I cherish.

Dad used to carry this big bunch of keys attached to his belt. When I was sitting in class, I would hear this clunking of the keys. I'd know that Dad had just walked up the stairs outside the room and I'd look out of the window in the door and see him walking past. If during any part of the day I wanted to talk to him, I knew he was there and of course he would make time for me. I could always rely on him to look after me.

I'd say Dad was a macho man; he was iron-chest-plated. He would deflect the bad things. He was always positive, and he believed in helping others.

He was London born and bred and his favourite football club was Millwall. By coincidence, in the same year that Dad was diagnosed, Millwall FC embarked on their partnership with Prostate Cancer UK. Mum and Dad got in touch with the charity and we all got involved, raising awareness and funds for prostate cancer. Millwall were great, really helpful, and they donated a lot to the cause.

I think that Millwall really started the campaign about prostate cancer in the football world. One in four black men and one in eight white men are affected. Football can still be quite a masculine game, and when you look around the stadium and see 10,000 people who are mostly men in there, you think, 'What is the likelihood of these people dying from prostate cancer?' The scale of the problem really brings it home. If you are diagnosed and you know about it, you have a chance. Unfortunately, for us the diagnosis was too late.

A lot of people say I have Dad in me, his inner strength. When you saw him start to deteriorate, start to use a walking stick, wheelchair and then be bedbound, unable to feel his legs, you could still see his inner qualities. He had this willingness never to give up. I hope I've learned that from him.

Thanks to our work for the charity, we spent a lot of quality time with each other after he stopped work. The whole family was involved.

That year Prostate Cancer UK and Sky Bet invited Dad to be guest of honour at the Championship play-offs, as an ambassador for the charity and to honour his achievements. We are from a humble background and there we were: first Dad on the pitch, shaking hands with all the players, then sitting down to watch the game from the royal box at Wembley. Dad had been on the pitch at Millwall too. Whenever I go to a game now, I think, 'My Dad walked on that pitch.' I also glance at the plaque on the wall with Dad's name on it. I always feel that he's with me, but especially when I see that plaque. Staff and senior members of both Millwall FC and Prostate Cancer UK came to his funeral and spoke about Dad. They were inspirational for Dad. Like a second medicine.

Because of how much I know about prostate cancer I knew that if during our campaigning work we could convince even one man to get checked and save just one life, we would have done our job. That's what inspired me to keep campaigning and to raise money for the charity.

That year in the UK, 10,000 men died from prostate cancer, though the figure is higher now. The charity ran a 10,000 challenge. You have to get sponsored to do 10,000 of something to raise money. Twice I collected 10,000 pennies. At the start of my fundraising my target was £1000 but we easily surpassed that.

The time from Dad being active to losing the use of his legs was six months. It was tough to watch this and see him stuck in one room. I wanted to spend time doing stuff with him, but he was bedbound. We couldn't play football or walk the dog. We couldn't even play chess.

Towards the end, it seemed as if every week we would be going to hospital for blood transfusions. Dad went to so many different hospitals and had so many treatments. I think I knew at the back of my mind that Dad would die. It's not something I was always thinking about, but when you see the effects of the treatment, the loss of hair, I knew that while he was saying he was fine on the outside, he was hurting on the inside.

Later on, because Dad had lost the use of his legs, I would help to hoist him in and out of bed. It wasn't nice that Dad couldn't do it himself, but I just had to just take it in my stride.

I think going to school was a break for me. It meant a change of scenery, seeing my mates, forgetting about the worry. I knew that when I went to school, I would come home at the end of the day and see Dad. Once I went on a day trip to France with school. Dad had a deterioration in his health, so he was meant to rush to hospital, but he stopped the paramedics taking him so that I could tell him about my day before he left.

I think Dad's illness helped me mature. I have been through so much as a kid and had to grow up quickly. I think I help around the house more. I think I have taken more individual responsibility.

Dad died in 2015. The loss is terrible but, as I say, he is always with me.

My friends have always been there for me too. I used to sell them Prostate Cancer UK badges and they still wear them on their blazers to this day. It's a reminder that they have supported me in what I've been through.

I've learned through what happened to Dad to live in the moment, to take every day as it comes. Sometimes there won't be a tomorrow. Every moment is special, so spend time with family and make memories. That's what they will cherish, and you will cherish them as well.

I know that if someone is suffering, it's worth taking time out of your schedule for them. One of the teachers at school organized a five-a-side football tournament to raise money to support us. Dad knew that we were raising money for the cause that he was dying from. It meant a lot.

Some people might see things differently, but I believe that if you see a loved one deteriorate, it's hard for you but harder for that person going through it. You will live to fight another day.

I am still raising money and I am close to £7000 now. One of Dad's friends at the school came round to the house to paint the ceiling and brought a big jar of 5p coins. My auntie and uncle own bakery and sandwich shops and they have collected money there. I have a written a blog about our family's journey 'My Man of Men', to help other people understand what the disease is like and why we so urgently need to beat it. As a teenager, I am full of ideas and drive to help make this happen. I write about prostate cancer from a teenager's point of view. I wrote recently, 'I am lucky that I have amazing parents who love me, even though one of them is not here with us.'

Increasingly, as a society we see influential people as the people with money or fame. We look at social media for that. The new generation, the younger generation, will sometimes be ignored and not seen as influential, but we have ideas that can be beneficial. We see the world with different eyes. We are open to new ideas. We are the future, the ones who will make a difference, so why not start listening to us now, rather than later? We need the platform to do this.

I would like to encourage teenagers, the next generation, to make a difference. There's a choice. Sit and play on your Xbox and watch TV or go into the world and make a change. That's an idea I hold.

I have seen such generosity and kindness in the way that people, including young people, have shown their loyalty and friendship to me. This is such a major thing. I know they care and they show empathy. Maybe the older generation is a bit stuck in their ways and not expecting to understand the newer generation's ideas and mindset. Teenagers just need the confidence and voice to put their ideas out there. We can work together, and if we stop one person dying, we will have achieved our purpose.

WILL

@ProstateUK

https://mymanofmen.
wordpress.com/tag/
william-kilgannon

"The new generation, the younger generation, will sometimes be ignored and not seen as influential, but we have ideas that can be beneficial. We see the world with different eyes."

MARTIN,

16, Glasgow, Scotland

"If you see someone being bullied or suffering, there's a natural part of you that thinks, 'That isn't right. That isn't fair.' It doesn't seem right not to intervene when things are wrong."

I work part-time in a pharmacy and I am so influenced by one of the pharmacists there, the way she approaches her work. It's not just the way she does her job, but how she goes out of her way to help people. She doesn't just recommend a good medicine; she really listens to the customer. Some people talk about pharmacy being incredibly corrupt and people going into it for the money. She does it because she loves her job.

I like the idea of changing the world, but I have always preferred the idea of doing that from a medical standpoint. I signed up with the Anthony Nolan project to donate stem cells, even though I hate needles. I'm waiting to hear if I'm a match. I genuinely hope I will be able to give something, even though it is a four-hour procedure which I would dread. If I was a pharmacist, this would benefit others because I would be helping them with their health, and it would help me because I would have a career, so everyone would win.

I believe one of the biggest things people need help with is their own health. They smoke too much, drink too much and die too young. My dad was diagnosed with the lung disease COPD but he didn't want to see his GP. He thought he would be being too much of a bother. I know that in the pharmacy people come in with bad situations. I want to be right there with people, giving advice.

One of the reasons I think I would be good at helping people is because I have had to get help myself. When I was in my second year at high school, I had to be referred for cognitive behavioural therapy (CBT) for depression. That was a difficult time. It was a time when I learned about taking care of myself. I know too many people are too shy and they can't admit to their GP they have problems. They don't think what's wrong is serious enough. I say if you have any problem at all, you should go and see someone. Even if you are just troubled, go and seek advice.

I joined Move On, an organization that supports teenagers, about two years ago. I was incredibly stressed because I'd been diagnosed with Asperger's. I had begun to have bad headaches and feel uncomfortable if I was in social spaces for too long. It's healthy to admit if you aren't able to handle something on your own. I was in a difficult place. I knew that if I didn't help myself then, moving ahead, I wouldn't be able to help others.

At school I belong to the Equality Group. I try to get help for people in the LGBT+ community and communities affected by racism. For a long time, there was no one there for people to talk to, confide their feelings in or explore this in any way.

The Equality Group gives people something to cling to if they need to report racism or if they're being bullied. People may not think there is racism, but you can get underlying comments. We can then tell Pastoral Care and say, 'You're not dealing with this issue.' We have the voices and the potential to keep hammering at people to have a positive influence in the school.

I'm now in the Pupil Parliament, a prefect in the school, and I'm hoping to fundraise for the Malawi Youth Leaders of Learning charity.

My parents want me to concentrate on my schoolwork and work experience, but to me it doesn't seem right not to intervene when things are wrong. If you see someone being bullied or suffering, there's a natural part of you that thinks, 'That isn't right. That isn't fair.' Even from my inner friendship circle, a lot of the response to what I do is passiveness. They ask, 'Why are you wasting your time?' I get that a lot. It's just who I am. It makes me want to help others more.

There's a general message now in society: you can do anything if you put your mind to it. I hold that message to myself quite closely. If I want people in our school and in our education system to have a fairer and easier time while they are there, then I will help them achieve this.

I have an inner belief that I can change things for the better and I think everybody can have that belief. All it takes is that simple turning on of a light switch in your head and you can believe that you can do something. Take a step back and ask yourself, 'How do I get there?' That's all it takes. It's that pathway that lets you get to places.

MARTIN

🐦 @moveonscotland

> "I have an inner belief that I can change things for the better and I think everybody can have that belief. All it takes is that simple turning on of a light switch in your head..."

MAYA,

13, London, England

"I wanted to use my bat mitzvah to fundraise and achieve something quite big. I was completely surprised when I raised £9000."

My parents are in the civil service and I grew up in India and Africa. This means I've lived in amazing houses while witnessing a lot of struggle. It feels right to me to give something back.

When you have a bat mitzvah, it's all about the process of becoming a Jewish adult. A lot of people are given presents, but I wanted to use my bat mitzvah to fundraise and achieve something quite big. I knew I didn't want any presents, so I walked 10,000 steps every day for a week – the recommended healthy number – and I asked people to sponsor me. They did this through a website that I set up. Most of it came from friends and family, and friends of friends.

I was completely surprised when I raised £9000. The money was matched by the government and it went to the Care International charity.

My main influence was when one of my parents saw the campaign film *Walk in Her Shoes*, which shows the challenges many women and girls face each day. This made me want to support children in other countries. I wanted to raise awareness of these issues and get people in my school involved.

I really tried to inspire people to raise money. One great thing about my Care International collection was that it was my grandparents' 50th wedding anniversary and they asked if their guests could donate to my fund instead of giving them presents.

One other good thing about the Care International fundraising was that it was easy to do and easy to get other people involved. I could fit it in with the school day. The headteacher was really enthusiastic. She asked students to come to school half an hour early and walk around the Astroturf to support me, with buckets on their heads, to symbolize children who have to carry water back and forth every day to their families.

For me, I was so pleased I could turn my bat mitzvah into something that was helping others. I felt as if I was doing something that meant something deeper for me. Everything we do as teenagers has an impact on someone. It's important that we believe in ourselves. We may be feeling moody and hormonal, but we are lucky even if we don't realize this, and we can have a positive effect on other people's lives. My fundraising showed me that just by doing something little every day you can totally achieve this and do something for children who aren't as fortunate as we are. It's so important that we all appreciate what we have.

MAYA

> "We are lucky even if we don't realize this, and we can have a positive effect on other people's lives."

MARYAM AND HADIQA,

17, Nelson,

Lancashire, England

> "We have tackled online hate, pushed for Fairtrade and worked in our communities. Young people don't realize how big an impact they can make."

As teenagers, we are subjected to a lot on social media. There's a lot of trolling. A lot of arguments and fights happen online, not face to face. The language used can be really hurtful. One of our group knew someone had written something about her and they denied they had done this. The message had been deleted and the teachers can't intervene.

We belong to a minority group and people comment on that. They link Muslims with terrorist groups. They say we've done things. They act on impulse, the spur of the moment. They get angry and because it's online we can't stand up to them. People hide behind a mask.

We are part of a young people's group called Positive Voices. Our parents or grandparents are from Pakistan, so we look at our history and see how we can make our community and young people's lives better.

The best thing we've done with Positive Voices is to be part of a computer hackathon called Peacehack to help them create an app to tackle online hate crime and keep us safe. A group of us travelled down to London to work with all these experts in computing. We were the youngest there and we had to talk and be open in front of a big room full of people we didn't know. It was intimidating.

One of the tasks before we went to London was to make a video about bullying and our experiences of people not being nice to us to give the computer experts information to work with.

A few of us were on the judging panel with people from Google and Facebook, and Dr Sue Black, the computer expert and campaigner. We listened to presentations about all the apps that the peacehackers had come up with. The main panel decided the winner was a group who wanted to alert people that they may be sending a message that could upset someone. It was a pop-up to make you think before you write something, which questioned, 'Are you sure you want to write this? It could be hurtful.'

Our group thought this was a good idea, but not the winning idea. We wanted to tackle the problem that someone puts something nasty on social media and then says to the teacher, 'It wasn't me. Someone hacked my system.' The idea of one of the hackers was for something that proved this wasn't true. People bully people and then hide behind technology by lying. We thought his idea would help us most, so we gave him a special prize of our own.

We think this would be a really important development for our generation. There are so many people online who feel they can be opinionated. They are teenagers and they think they can say what they want. And they can do this without revealing their identity. This is cyberbullying.

Positive Voices has given us both a lot of confidence. There is a stereotype that if you are from a deprived community, you will amount to nothing. We both want to amount to something. Maryam wants to work in clinical neuropsychology for children and adolescents. She suffers with anxiety so will be able to understand and communicate with them. It is an important time to go into this – everyone is discussing mental health issues in young people. Hadiqa wants to become a barrister. Working in criminal law will be her way of having an impact on the world, through a system created to maintain order and peace.

We feel that a lot of young people are interested in clothes and what they look like and they haven't looked beyond that. It can be good to indulge yourself, but looks aren't forever. The Kardashians are not always going to look like they do. Young people don't realize how big an impact they can make. Before Peacehack we didn't think we could make big impact. We didn't think we could speak in public. Since then we've been involved in a conference on radicalization with university students. We were 15- and 16-year-olds talking to students. We work with the local town council. We push for Fairtrade. It's amazing what you do when you try. You can get involved with groups, or just continue with your life and think about the world and live in a good way. Your life is well spent if you help your community and help put everyone on the path to happiness. This is what makes us happy.

The more you get involved, the more difference you can make. The world has a different perspective than if you sit and watch *Love Island* on TV, go to bed and go to sleep. There's so much more to do and explore in the world.

HADIQA AND MARYAM

@maryamalixd

"There is a stereotype that if you are from a deprived community, you will amount to nothing. We both want to amount to something. Your life is well spent if you help your community and help put everyone on the path to happiness."

ADAM,

15, Clondalkin, Ireland

"When Dad falls, I always rush in automatically to help him and get him up, but it's heart-breaking. I think, 'That's my dad on the floor.'"

When I was 7, my dad had a hernia operation which went wrong, and it all went downhill from there. He ended up in chronic pain and he's been very, very sick ever since. He sometimes stops breathing at night; he has fallen downstairs and fallen in the shower. When he falls, I will always rush in automatically to help him and get him up. I always make sure he's all right, but it's heart-breaking. I think, 'That's my dad on the floor.'

It was a big shock when he was first ill, but I had no idea what was happening. To begin with, I had no idea what chronic pain was. Now I'm 15 and I understand it all. It's pain in every bone, muscle and joint. Pain in your whole body.

Before Dad was ill, we used to go to the park; he used to bring us into his work where he was in security. He took us to football matches and would come to my football matches. He'd been in the army reserves since he was 15 or 16 and served most of his years in the military police. I was so used to him being healthy. We were both active together.

Then he had the operation and since then it's been tough most days. It's really good when he has a good day and he's happy interacting with us all. If he's not feeling down, he'll watch telly and go to the shops on his mobility scooter. On bad days he feels really, really bad. It's painful for me when he's suffering because he's my dad. If I saw someone else in the same situation, it would be sad but not as sad.

On good days I just want things to stay as they are; on bad days I wish we could go back to the past, but of course that's not possible.

I help my mum all I can. My dad always comes first. I will say to my mum, 'You can go off for an hour or two and I'll wait with Dad.' Everything revolves around him. If my friends are going to the cinema or out for the day, it will depend what state my dad's in and whether my mum's in whether I go. I shower him, help him walk up the stairs if he thinks he's going to fall, help him with his medication, remind him what time to take it.

I love soccer and Gaelic football. I had to give up soccer because of caring for him, but I play Gaelic football for Clondalkin Round Towers. I'm strong, fast and agile, just as he was when he was young.

Being a carer has definitely changed me. My family and family friends all say, 'You're doing a brilliant job.' I was always a kind and helpful person, but winning Young Carer of the Year has really boosted my confidence.

Family Carers Ireland and Mark, who's my Gaelic football manager, have also been a big help. They've realized what I have gone through. If I'm frustrated or angry, Mark talks to me and helps me forget about the bad day. Local politicians have supported me, and one councillor gave me an award from the South Dublin County Council. The bad thing is that since I won Young Carer and had a lot of attention, some people at school are really jealous and they're giving me a hard time. They won't leave me alone. I don't want to fight – I hate fighting – but they go out to fight. I have recently moved school. No one at the new school knew I was doing a caring role. Now I've been on telly and the whole school knows what I do. You can't tell anyone if you're being bullied because you get called a snitch. Being a teenager is difficult. It's difficult in general.

I would still say that winning the award is the best thing that's ever happened to me. I have been recognized for what I'm doing. People say to me, 'How much did you get paid for winning?' but it's not about payment – it's about recognition.

I think still the school doesn't always understand. They ask, 'Adam, why are you late?' I tell them I'm having to help my dad.

When I'm older, I would like to do something to do with caring. Every Saturday morning I help coach 4–7-year-olds in Gaelic football, which is fun, and recently I helped out with a cool camp of fun games for younger kids.

I'd advise anyone in my position to keep up the good work and don't ever give up. Being a carer and being recognized for what I've done has made me feel really good. It was an ordinary school day. I got home, and they said, 'Young Carer of the Year: you've won it!' I just broke out into tears.

I think one benefit of being a carer is that I'm more open to people. There was a lovely lady on my old road and I used to say to her, 'How are you doing, Josie? Can I give you a hand?' Even on snowy days, I would run to the shops and bring her milk and teabags, dropping them in to her. I would keep an eye on her so I knew she was OK, even though she has a family.

Life can be tough, but I think if anyone is having a difficult time they should tell their mum and dad, someone they trust. The people who are there for them. Knowing you have people on your side is better than having no one there. Much better.

Talking to people is what makes me feel better. That and kicking the ball in Gaelic football. I can kick that ball so hard it releases everything.

ADAM

🐦 @CarersIreland
📘 Family Carers Ireland

"Being a carer has definitely changed me. My family and family friends all say, 'You're doing a brilliant job.' I'd advise anyone in my position to keep up the good work and don't ever give up."

JAC,

14, Merthyr Tydfil,

Wales

"One of my friends has learned to stick up for himself and he's learned that from me."

Once in year 5* I had to get taken out of the lesson to calm down because this boy was being mean to my brother. I was so angry. I was ranting about why he shouldn't have done what he did. I was glad when the boy was excluded, but I realize how stupid it was that I got so angry.

I don't know why, but certain things make me angry. In class when we don't have time to finish something, I usually get annoyed. I feel like everyone should have enough time to write everything out. I get angry when people take stuff without asking. If I get too angry, I cry from anger. I used to punch my pillows, or I'd shout really loudly. I would never hit, but I would shout. I would get the blame when things went wrong because I was so angry, and sometimes people would tease me about it.

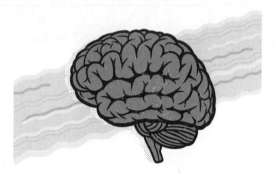

Mindfulness was recommended to me because of my anger and now I find it easier to control. I would go to the teacher who taught mindfulness and we did these breathing techniques that really helped me. I was really sad when the teacher left. She was one of the nicest teachers I have known.

---

*　　Ages 9–10.

I think it's much better that I'm not as angry now, because I can talk through my problems. Before, even when I'd calmed myself down, people would say, 'What's wrong?' and I couldn't explain it well. Now I calm down super easy and I can talk about my emotions and why I was angry.

With my level of anger, at one stage I'd thought, 'Nothing's going to calm me down,' but mindfulness and my friends have helped me change for the better.

My best friend is the smart one: he's the brains, I'm the brawn. He's really, really smart. If anyone's mean to him, usually it's me who gets annoyed. He laughs it off. He doesn't talk back to people, but I talk back. I really want to punch them, but I don't because I would end up in trouble, but I do sound like I want to.

In year 7 and 8[†] people would say I was weird, but I know that doesn't matter. I'm me and I'm not here to please everyone else. We are only supposed to change to be a better person than we already are. You can't change yourself because some people don't like you. Always some people will be friends with you if other people aren't, and I am thankful for my friends. I wouldn't be the person I am without them. They have helped me to improve to be a better person. I know there will always be someone by my side.

My uncle passed away and I was very close to him. He was a mechanic and now I want to be a mechanic to carry on his work. When he died, I needed people to support me. Having more friends may mean you're popular, but for me it's always quality

---

[†]   Ages 11–13.

over quantity. You need friends you can trust from the bottom of your heart, who you can be yourself with.

I'm going to try to help other people in the future. With experiencing what I have experienced, I will be in a good position to help. That's the type of person I am. Treat people how you'd like to be treated. If someone bullies someone else, if they say they are ugly or fat or weird, over the years I've realized it's OK to ignore it. If they have a problem, they have to deal with it. Opinions come from people who don't know the real person.

I have a gay friend and people make fun of him. I just say, 'Just back off'. They think they are all smart; they just want an argument, but I argue back for my friend's right to love who he wants. When people take the mick, I find that disgusting. I hate homophobia. People say you support it so you're gay yourself, but I just want to support my friends. I think, 'Why are you hating a person for that?' I think if you don't want to help someone, just leave them alone. I don't want to hurt people's feelings; I want to help people for the better. I want to be a force for good, better and stronger in the mind and heart. If you stick up for what you know is good and right, you will automatically be better than the bully.

I hope people will copy my example. I think I'm doing things that are good for people. One of my friends has learned to stick up for himself and he's learned that from me. No matter how much you try, no matter what you say, I won't stop sticking up for my friends. If I know what's said is not right, I will always stick up for them.

Because of some people's personalities, they can't handle what they are going through, so I need to help them. I know they can't deal with it. Earlier, in English, they were being mean to my friend and I said, 'Can you shut up – he doesn't want to talk to you.' I was so annoyed at that. It's interesting that no one says anything mean to me.

I used to be worried about my anger, but now I'm glad I have it. Otherwise I wouldn't be able to stick up for anyone. I thank my anger for that.

JAC

> "I used to be worried about my anger, but now I'm glad I have it. Otherwise I wouldn't be able to stick up for anyone. I thank my anger for that."

LILI,

13, London, England

"Being a teenager is a good time to develop the skills to help others and those skills will stay with you for your whole life."

I feel like I'm very different to how society wants females to be. For example, I play football at a competitive level, which is always considered to be a boys' sport. I have never really got into make-up and stuff like that. I have thought sometimes, 'What if they think I'm weird?' but I can't impress everyone, so there's no point trying. People will always have something negative to say, so it's important to be yourself and just do what you want anyway. I think people who criticize should start finding confidence within themselves first. If you become strong and are happy within yourself, you can make others happy.

My mum always says be a glass-half-full person. Try to look on the positive side; even when things seem bad, there's always a way out of it. Try to get through it; look at all the good sides.

One aspect that teenagers might feel a little bit unhappy about is that sometimes they are not taken seriously by adults and that isn't a very nice feeling. I think adults should try to remember what it was like to be younger. Sometimes we will have to learn from our own mistakes; sometimes we have to learn from other people's; but we often need to experience things and live through them first.

I liked being in primary school because no one judged you. You could be yourself. You could wear what you want, and it didn't matter. I found at the beginning of secondary school I started feeling, 'Oh gosh, this person thinks

I'm this or that.' I worried too much about what people thought.
I became friends with some people I probably wouldn't be friends
with now. I'm happy I experienced that because I learned a lot not
to be influenced and changed by other people. It was very helpful
to go through that.

I feel like I'm the sort of person to experience something and
learn from that, rather than be told what to think or feel, then
willing myself to be different.

I enjoyed my time with the first friendship group, but I felt that
after school I didn't want to get into trouble. It wasn't nice to be
scared that I would be in trouble. These people are still my friends,
but I need to make my foundation strong for the future and do the
important things.

I learned about the important things quite young. My dad's
from Ethiopia. I remember going there when I was quite young
and seeing lots of children who have no parents. In fact, they have
no one. They are homeless, and the police are not nice to them.
They were begging constantly and trying to sell small items such
as chewing gum and tissues, and the police were hounding them
and moving them away on the street. I remember one boy who was
very small with a very deep voice. Mum said that maybe he was
malnourished and couldn't afford the food to grow.

More recently, I remember giving a child some money and my
dad asked him what his situation was. His dad hadn't been there,
so there had just been him and his mum. Then his mum had died.
It was very sad that the police were not helping him. I thought
it would be really great if someone would volunteer to help
him. If I was in his position, I would be really grateful for that.

It gave me this feeling that is so important to work together to improve things.

I remember when the Ebola outbreak happened in Sierra Leone, knowing that many people wouldn't get the help they needed, I felt that I wanted to make a difference. I decided to do something. So in year 6* my friends and I raised money through a page on the internet and a cake sale. We raised £800. This showed me how much we could achieve if we tried.

At the moment, together with a couple of friends I'm trying to make people aware of the issue of domestic violence. We have talked to a charity called Tender, which works with children to try to prevent unhealthy relationships. We wanted to create a presentation to show our class, so we went to Tender and they gave us some tips on what we should include.

With domestic violence, it's hard for people to speak out if they are in a relationship. They might not want to accept that a relationship is unhealthy. It can be really hard to leave and they might need help but not realize it or not know where to go. That's where the charity steps in.

It's important for young people to know the signs. If they start a family and the relationship isn't working out, it can be so hard for the child. I've learned to put myself in other people's shoes and this makes me want to help people more. I think that being a teenager is a good time to develop the skills to help others and those skills will stay with you for your whole life.

---

*   Ages 10–11.

My mum is a doctor and works with survivors of torture. I think her job is a really great cause. I think it's always important to help others, to be part of a community and socially active. Then we can be true to ourselves, help others and have good relationships. It's the best way to be.

LILI

"I think it's always important to help others, to be part of a community and socially active. Then we can be true to ourselves and have good relationships."

TIAN,

14, London, England

"It's good to find others who are adopted, and we can help each other. This is hard to talk about to people who don't understand."

In the past I have had a rough time fitting in. A lot of my friends know who their parents are, but I was adopted. I do have a lot of support, and this makes me want to help other people who don't have that same support.

My adoptive parents give me a lot of support. I'm Chinese but I was born in England. My birth mother was at university here. I would like to meet her one day. I think she made a good decision. Where she lived was quite traditional, in China near North Korea. When she was a student here, she met my birth father, but she was not in position to look after me, so she left me at a foster home. People think she went back home.

I find that it's good to find others who are adopted, and we can help each other. There are counsellors, but they don't fully understand.

When I'm in sixth form,* I want to see if there are any opportunities to help people who are adopted. It's quite a tough subject, hard to talk about to people who don't understand. Since I am adopted, I can share my experiences with other people. There might be charity work I can do.

I think what helps teenagers to make changes in society is making sure they know that people around them will respect them and give them the power to do something about their situation. I didn't have the power to change my situation when I was adopted. I could have found that tough, but then I realized it was a mental thing. Even in a tough situation, you have a path that shows you have power. If you find someone who has been through the same

---

*   Ages 16–18.

situation as you, you can talk it through with them and will feel more confident that you have power to change how you feel.

If someone is depressed but has the support of people, this can give them a way to change. It's very hard but there's always a way to do it.

What's helped me is to have a close friend. We push each other to do well. If you know you can talk to someone, it gives you a warm feeling. This can help you get over something that's getting you down. You need to have the confidence to go and tell someone how you feel, because modern-day society is hard. You don't want things to build up and the depression gets worse.

If one of my friends had a conflict with someone, I feel as if I'm someone who can give advice to them to help them stay friends. When you've managed to achieve something like this, it opens your mind. Knowing you can sort something out gives you the confidence to do this again.

I'm someone people go to for help. I ask my friends, 'Are you OK? Do you want to talk about things?' I like to express different ways to help, but you do need to be able to look after yourself so that you don't get emotionally drained. Then, when you feel strong, you can help other people. You are technically carrying the burden of their problems as well – you get an insight into what they're going through. I think I like helping others because I'm adopted.

For some reason it's given me an intuition, a different way of seeing relationships.

TIAN

"If you find someone who has been through the same situation as you, you can talk it through with them and feel more confident that you have power to change how you feel."

EVELYN,

14, London, England

"I see people struggling and I can relate to them. If you want a better world with more love in it and more people being kind instead of ignoring other people's hurt, empathy is the key."

Everyone has a hard time in high school. You can have the most accepting family, you can have all the confidence in the world, but still people at school will give you a hard time. While no one has it easy, it's really important to help those who are obviously struggling.

At my school they say they accept everyone, but it takes a lot to change hearts and minds. I do what I can to spread tolerance.

For me, it's an empathy thing. I see people struggling and I can relate to them. If you want a better world, with more love in it, and more people being kind instead of ignoring other people's hurt, empathy is the key.

It's easy to think there are lots of other people out there helping out and doing the work, but there are a lot of people not being helped. There are lots of issues not being touched on enough.

LGBT+, Black Lives Matter, the women's movement…they say there's not enough help for them and I think that is valid and true. I've helped out at a homeless shelter and that's what the LGBT+ people told me there.

I'm bisexual and for me the most important issue to deal with is the homophobia in school. I am in the LGBT+ group and we organize staff meetings to explain to staff about students being targeted. Sometimes the teachers are afraid of going against this. I find there's a lot of stigma around. People say being bisexual is a phase or that it's not a real thing. They say we are people who are just experimenting. It's belittling. I'm fortunate to have friends and family who are accepting of who I am. We have members of our group who are transgender, and I would say our school community's acceptance of them is imperfect. You can have rainbows on your badges and your flags, but acceptance in your heart is different.

We have a place for our group to meet at lunchtime and that's so important. You can go there and eat your lunch, talk and relax. Everyone's calm. Sometimes you have people blasting in who are trying to be funny in front of their friends – people who are uneducated. It's not their fault. If someone doesn't understand something and they are a bully, they are going to target you.

There's definitely a mould that teens feel they need to fit into, even for the LGBT+ community. Stereotypical moulds about the music we like and what our wardrobes will look like. All of this is what we're supposed to buy into, but you don't have to do that. It's important we are all ourselves.

Outside of school, you can see YouTube videos of people having a great time, which can feel encouraging, but YouTube can also be used the other way: for people to spread hatred and create stereotypes.

At this age everyone can be influenced. Social media generally just makes everything more extreme. It makes people who are out and proud happier and more open, but if someone feels bad things about their body image or about their race or whatever other issue, it will make those feelings stronger too. There are films of people talking about coming out which have no swearing, no nudity, just talking about being gay or being trans with no adult content, and they would have helped me.

If someone is struggling to come out, I would say don't come out to anyone unless you are in a safe space and until you have completely come out to yourself. If you are ready to come out, then no one can stop you from being who you are. If you say, 'I might be this,' they'll say, 'That's not you.' The main thing is to know you are in a safe space, so you can be completely open to yourself. Then you can go on to help other people and help them feel safer. If you have people in school who are being themselves, it can give others hope that they can be themselves one day. Even a badge can make a difference: a Black Lives Matter badge, a rainbow badge, a badge that says 'let women be women'.

Life can be difficult for teenagers. If someone thinks girls can't have armpit hair, they will watch a celebrity or YouTuber talk about how girls shouldn't have to shave, or they do have to shave, and that will reinforce how they feel or move towards  them changing their mind. So social media can create problems, but it can also create really good things, helping people to start companies and become more confident. It can go both ways.

As a teenager, you tend to change who you are quite a lot. People who are confident and are themselves get targeted by other kids. Anyone who's slightly different, even if it's just that your hair looks weird – anything can make you a target. Many people will be overwhelmed about this; it makes people want to go with the crowd. If you are part of the mould and just fit into society, people don't target you, but if you want to be yourself, people will.

Definitely, things are improving. I know that my mum didn't grow up in a house where it was OK to be gay, but in our house now we have rainbow flags. We put them away before my gran comes round, though!

EVELYN

"Social media can create problems, but it can also create really good things, helping people to become more confident. It can go both ways."

DILLON,

18, Malibu,

California, USA

"I took a tour of an LGBT youth homeless shelter in LA and met these kids who were trying to get job interviews, but they didn't have any fashionable clothing to wear. I set up a non-profit to help them."

My favorite thing to do is take out my outfit every morning and lay it on my bed. Dressing up every day makes me feel confident. When it hit me that homeless young kids can't do that – that they don't have that privilege – it was a surreal moment.

I took a tour of an LGBT youth homeless shelter in LA in 2014 and met these kids who were trying to get job interviews, but they didn't have any fashionable clothing to wear if they got them. I knew I wanted to help them. I asked myself, 'I have always been interested in fashion. How can I take that interest of mine and turn it into a solution to benefit my own community?'

Although I liked fashion, my level of interest never really exploded until I felt I had an obligation to help. I'm creative in my head but not so much with my hands; I'm not very good at drawing or painting. At that stage I had never used a sewing machine. So I started watching YouTube videos to try to teach myself some basic skills.

I began to improve, but it was a bit of a struggle. For a long time, I didn't have the physical skills to do what I wanted to do, which was frustrating. I've never had any formal training, but now I have developed some tricks that enable me to make alterations to old clothes to make them look great again.

When I first went back to the shelter and delivered some clothing I had been working on, I didn't expect the reaction I got. It was a simple gesture, but I realized how my little effort made a big impact on their confidence. Heartbroken, I was determined to help more people than just those at this shelter. I wanted to help other homeless people who are wearing out-of-style, damaged clothes and restore their self-empowerment.

I find that when I help people directly in the streets, often they get very emotional. One woman I gave a jacket to said it was the first jacket she'd had for six months and she started to cry. Four years later, I'm still crushed remembering this moment and it humbles me.

I think part of the emotional reaction I get is because someone has taken the time to do something for them, especially if they are young and homeless. Their parents and family have neglected them. They are people living on streets with no one else to care for them, no family to support them or rely on. The fact that someone has shown them some care and given them some time makes them feel wanted again, dignified.

I decided to take this venture seriously and set up what's known as a 501(c)(3) non-profit. The clothes I use are donations which come to me in all different ways. The first is through individual donations: people will send donations directly. The second is from corporate partnerships: I'm currently working with Abercrombie & Fitch. They send me merchandise to use, things from their outlet locations and distribution facilities that are samples or surplus stock. I also partner up with other non-profits or homeless shelters who already have donations that are unusable. I try to minimize any shopping, but sometimes I buy items from thrift stores at cut price that are interesting and cool and inspire my work.

My parents have been influential in helping me develop the organization, especially my mum. She drives me several hours back and forth from home to downtown LA where there are a lot of shelters. My dad is a lawyer, so he has helped me with a lot with the legal aspects of running a company.

I think that unless you have the experience of seeing a problem for yourself, you don't realize the little things about people that are such disadvantages. I would never have thought this need for clothing was a problem in my own community. I wouldn't have done anything if I didn't know the problem was there; a lot of kids just aren't exposed to situations like these.

A lot of schools in LA require you to do volunteering before you graduate. Often the volunteering is not connected to people's hobbies and interests, especially if people have not been exposed to real-world problems. This means they are getting a negative perspective of volunteering as something that's boring, so they won't want to do it. Yes, they are volunteering, but it is mundane and they are not enjoying it.

For me, I have a hobby that I can use to help other people. That's a big difference – forcing kids to do something is very different from encouraging them to use their own interests to generate a local impact.

Time, however, is an ongoing struggle for me. It's really challenging to go to school for seven hours, then do three hours of homework, studying for tests, and run a non-profit. I just graduated high school and will be attending college, at Washington University in St. Louis, where I'll be minoring in the Businesses of Social Impact. When I move to college in the fall, I'm going to bring my company with me. Some shelters that I currently work with in LA have chapters and divisions in Missouri. There's a lot of poverty in St. Louis, so I will be busy making collections there.

I get emails from people around the world who've heard about what I do and want to take it to their own town, so I hope to build a network of volunteers who want to start their own version. Right now, I'm working with someone in Chicago to pilot the program. Recently, I had someone contact me from prison, saying would I help released convicts get jobs. It is fascinating how people from all walks of life are able to relate to my journey and this encourages me to go out and develop what I am doing even further and motivate other young people to also go out and begin their social entrepreneurship efforts.

I hope one day my company will become so large that a lot of clothing companies will rethink or re-evaluate their thoughts on corporate social responsibility. There's a kind of stigma about how big businesses are driven to succeed and don't care about anything other than profit, but that mentality is changing and I hope to become a part of that change. I would never have thought that such an influential company as Abercrombie & Fitch would be interested in supporting my grassroots project. It's interesting that companies are coming forward to help people in their own communities and it's exciting to see how businesses are evolving. Currently, a lot of companies discard or even burn their unwanted clothes. What I have developed is an innovative way to use what they already have but don't necessarily need.

I think it's really important to let kids know that just because you're young, you don't need to be intimidated if you want to help others. I have had so many people saying, 'We don't want to partner with you; we don't believe in what you are doing.' It's really upsetting, dispiriting. You need to have resilience. There is always someone out there will support your idea. You never know where your idea will take you, who it will help, or who it will inspire.

The youth are the next generation; it's never too early to go out into the world and create change.

DILLON

@sew_swag

www.sewswag.org

"Forcing kids to do something is very different from encouraging them to use their own interests to generate an impact. You never know where your idea will take you, who it will help or who it will inspire."

8...

WELL, WHAT DID YOU THINK?

Read this book and you'll find it hard to deny that teens can be a force for good in the world. A teenager can take an idea, mix it with their personal brand of willpower and passion, and make their own lives and the lives of those around them better and brighter.

Others believe this too.

Science shows that teenagers are quick learners, creative and open to new ideas. In one survey, nine out of ten said they wanted careers that would make a difference and tackle social issues, by helping animals, saving lives or tackling homelessness.*

'I used to feel helpless and unable to play my part,' says charity worker Taybah Begum, now 20. 'I thought if I attended events, I would be the only young person there. I thought this large-scale kind of work was for older people and that I was not capable.' Then, at 19, Taybah became a global campaigns agency administrator, helping with projects on air pollution and on poverty in Kenya. She now works as a fundraising officer for a humanitarian aid charity, helping Palestinians in need.

I've organized events that raise awareness for the cause and a skydive challenge to raise funds for our education aid programme. Through my work experiences, I've learnt that teenagers give up their time and put in a lot of effort with a clear vision. I know that young people will shape the future.

---

*   Survey of 1246 UK 9–18-year-olds, August 2017, commissioned by Engineering UK. See https://www.engineeringuk.com/news-media/young-people-demand-jobs-that-make-a-difference.

Researcher Laura Partridge[†] says, 'We really do underestimate teenagers and young people and, when we speak to them, there are so many doing great things; so many have a culture of "giving back".'

She adds:

> I think a lot of what the media does in order to attract readers gives teenagers a bad press. A lot of what they do is stereotyping: for instance presenting a small group involved in criminal activities and painting a picture that's a larger threat than it really is. To them, to report a rise in youth violence is what's interesting and the nuance gets lost.

Meanwhile Lisa Zimmermann, who's spent ten years working with teenage activists at the Integrate UK charity in Bristol, said that the charity was actually co-founded with a group of 12 young activists. She says, 'They knew what they wanted to change in society and articulated this in a way that, as one former government minister put it, "could not be ignored".'

She continues:

> Over the years I've watched the charity grow as more and more teenagers become involved and gradually take on roles with increasing responsibility within the organization.

[†]   Laura Partridge is one of the authors of *Teenagency: How young people can create a better world*, London: RSA, 2018. Available at www.thersa.org/discover/publications-and-articles/reports/teenagency-how-young-people-can-create-a-better-world.

I've been amazed by their ability to identify issues and offer solutions and, yes, in an unusual way.

After a friend of theirs left for Syria at the age of 15, they developed two powerful lesson plans around grooming for radicalisation, gang and drug culture and child sexual exploitation. Their energy and confidence is infectious. I know our young activists can lead a movement for positive change and create a society that is fair and equal – they give all of us hope for the future.

Academics are on the side of the teens. Frances E. Jensen, neurologist at the University of Pennsylvania explains: 'Teenage brains have more synaptic connections than adult ones, which makes them highly impressionable. It's a period of huge opportunity.'[‡] Professor Sarah-Jayne Blakemore, in her book *Inventing Ourselves: The Secret Life of the Teenage Brain*, writes that adolescents have a greater capacity for change than adults because their brain is developing. She says: 'Adolescence is a time of heightened creativity and novel thinking, energy and passion.'[§]

[‡] Forster, K. (2015) 'Secrets of the teenage brain.' *The Observer*, 25 January 2015. Accessed on 4/12/2018 at https://www.theguardian.com/lifeandstyle/2015/jan/25/secrets-of-the-teenage-brain.

[§] Blakemore, S.-J. (2018) *Inventing Ourselves: The Secret Life of the Teenage Brain*. London: Doubleday.

Everyone knows that teens are strongly influenced by their friends, and this is often presumed to be a bad thing. The truth is that it can be a good thing too, as many of the stories in this book show. The influence can be positive, with friends encouraging each other to behave with compassion and generosity. Similarly, teens are often branded risk-takers, but risks can be good – the route to growth and change.

As you've seen, for the stars of this book, age is definitely an advantage. As Josie, 16, from the USA, says:

> I see how teens are rising up... We can come together and be stronger. Once you start identifying the problems and noticing what's happening around you, there's a fire inside you that gets brighter and brighter. We will put out that fire only by making change.

And Lucy, who's 17, from England, says:

> This is a great point to look around and think, 'Is this the kind of world I want to grow up in?' I think my age has helped me. Everything seemed so clear to me. I didn't let myself overthink what I was doing. The change was important to me and this let me shut out the criticism.

Betty, 13, from the Netherlands believes:

> If your heart is in it and you try your best, you will get to places and do things in your life… Some people think they can't change things because they are just one person…but if everyone did one small thing there would be a massive change. It's as simple as that.

And someone else who sees things simply is Will, who's 15, from London. 'I would like to encourage teenagers, the next generation, to make a difference,' he says. 'There's a choice. Sit and play on your Xbox and watch TV or go into the world and make a change.'

Trisha, who's 18, from the USA, also believes there is a choice to be made:

> All teens are passionate about something: music, art, science, law, politics, friends, communities, families… As teenagers, so much of life is in front of you. We can take that feeling of 'I am invincible. Let me try to do something,' and channel it. If we channel it into negative thinking, the results can be appalling. Channel it into something positive, the results can be great.

If you've been encouraged by these teens and others, here are some tips to get you on your way…

9...

YOUR TOOLKIT

Some people within this book are making changes to their own lives. For them, their toolkit will be willpower, support from others and a deep desire for something new.

If you are looking to change something in your community, here are some thoughts for you:

- Believe in your idea, or no one else will.

- Make your idea simple – you'll only have a second to attract someone's attention on social media.

- Be truthful, accurate and well informed.

- Be creative, bold and memorable – but don't exaggerate.

- Try to emphasize the positive. Why is what you want to achieve a good thing? People are more likely to support a campaign if they're convinced of the benefits and think they can help make a difference.

- If you want to attract well-known supporters, up-and-coming vloggers and influencers can be a big help; you don't necessarily need to reach big celebrity names. Look for influencers who are authentic and have the same values, passion or beliefs as you. This is more important than attracting those who just have a big following.

- Being part of an online community can be a great way of getting support. It can turn into a kind of online family.

- Online petitions have been tremendously successful in forcing those in power to change their decisions.

- Always get someone else to check what you have written, to make sure it's clear and there are no mistakes.

- Don't underestimate the importance of visuals: check what has worked for other campaigns when it comes to successful photos, logos or cartoons. Videos should be captioned and no longer than 90 seconds.

- Don't forget to get creative with all the great free online tools available, including editing apps for visuals.

- You may personally use Snapchat, Instagram and YouTube, for instance, but getting coverage on TV, radio, newspapers, Facebook and Twitter is important too.

- Hashtags work wonders and create the sense of a movement.

- Having a coherent 'brand' for your online campaign is important. If you post about anything and everything, people will be confused about what to expect from you.

- Join pages and groups to reach others who are likely to care about your mission. Don't just promote your campaign to your friends.

- Never underestimate the importance of hard work. Everyone in this book is focused and motivated to achieve their goal.

- Be prepared for criticism. Criticism can be your friend; you can use it to refine your argument. Criticism can fuel your motivation as long as you don't give up. Prove the critics wrong!

- Read the stories of the campaigners in this book who have begun to make big changes in the areas they believe in. Their experiences could fuel your imagination.

And, to quote Nike,
'JUST DO IT!'

ACKNOWLEDGEMENTS

Thank you to the splendid Amy Lankester-Owen and the team at Jessica Kingsley Publishers for all your help with this book. Thanks too to the fantastic teens from all over the world who have so generously shared their stories and selfies. Thanks to everyone who has helped me to find interviewees and guide my ideas into place (full list overleaf). Special editorial thanks to Liz Barron, Sarah Neville and Eileen Maybin; and thanks to my agent Jane Judd, Jessica Kingsley (never forgotten!) and my lovely family.

Special thanks to:

Andy Kaye

Ann Rappaport

Anne Metcalfe

Ashleigh Wilmot

Barbara Reissner

Barrie, Emile and Alison Chi

Caroline Heldman

Claire Armitstead

Connor Magennis

Emma Tallamy, The Stars Foundation

Family Carers Ireland, Catherine Cox

Fixers

Frances Alagiah

Gail Black, Alcoa of Australia,
Nature Bridge Scholarships

Global Girl Media especially Amie Williams,
Heidi Basch-Harod, Jasmine Jaisinghani

Helen Robinson

India Baird, Rock Girl

Jane Butler

Kirstie Brewer

Kurt Lee

Laura Polenco

Liz Millar

Lola Phoenix

Loretta Magennis

Malawi Girl Guides Association,
especially Khama Ziyabu

Marine Society & Sea Cadets,
Kayleigh Lewis

Marsden Heights Community College,
especially Mashuq Hussain OBE

Martin Crook

Martine Parry

Miki Mielonen

The Move On team

Nick Lewis

Nicki Ryan of the Free2B Alliance

Nicole Socher

Orsola de Castro,
Fashion Revolution @Fash_Rev

Pen Y Dre High School,
especially Sarah Hunnisett

Pip Ainsworth

Prostate Cancer UK, especially
Dianne Stradling and Gary Haines

Rose and Sarah – thank you for your support

Saffron Cooksey

Samantha Bandak

Sam Shaw

Sarah Hymas

Stephen Griffith,
Copenhagen Youth Project

Stoke Newington School, especially
Francis Ebeneli

Dr Sue Black, OBE

Susan Paley

The Children's Society,
especially Charlie Coombes

The Penny, Sue and Pip tea and cake group

Vivien Fowle

World Association of Girl Guides and
Girl Scouts, especially Grace Tam,
Megan Hunt, Ruth Stone

Read more **JKP** books:

Dyslexia is My Superpower (Most of the Time)

Margaret Rooke

Forewords by Professor Catherine Drennan
and Loyle Carner

ISBN 978 1 78592 299 2

eISBN 978 1 78450 606 3

Creative, Successful, Dyslexic

23 High Achievers Share Their Stories

Margaret Rooke

Foreword by Mollie King

ISBN 978 1 78592 060 8 (Paperback)

ISBN 978 1 84905 653 3 (Hardback)

eISBN 978 1 78450 163 1

The Mental Health and Wellbeing Workout for Teens

Skills and Exercises from ACT and CBT
for Healthy Thinking

Paula Nagel

Illustrated by Gary Bainbridge

ISBN 978 1 78592 394 4

eISBN 978 1 78450 753 4